STEPPING UP

Make Decisions That Matter

TIMOTHY DOBBINS

Collins

An Imprint of HarperCollinsPublishers

HarperCollins books may be purchased for educational, business, or sales promotional use. For information, please write to: Special Markets Department, HarperCollins Publishers, 10 East 53rd Street, New York, NY 10022.

Designed by Joe Rutt

Library of Congress Cataloging-In-Publication has been applied for.

ISBN-13: 978-0-06-082373-3
ISBN-10: 0-06-082373-9

06 07 08 09 10 DIX/RRD 10 9 8 7 6 5 4 3 2 1

what I admire about you is your

__Strength.__

You also have __will__.

With out these two (2) elements there will be no success.

__Stay focused__ Know you have an. (Angle /Devil) that will make all things work for you.

A beacon is a light that will guide you. But you must be in control of your ship.

November 2009

Ship [signature]

STEPPING UP

Dedication

With deep gratitude and affectionate appreciation for those clients and parishioners, who over the years have stepped up and allowed me to practice what I teach.

Most importantly, *Stepping Up* is dedicated **to you** the reader, who by holding this book in your hands already possess the desire to step up and make decisions that matter: and matter for the common good. What I want to say to you, Henry David Thoreau says best:

"'Tis the
good **reader**
that makes the
good book
. . . in every book
he finds
passages
which seem
confidences
or **asides**
hidden from
all else and
unmistakably meant
for his **ear.**"

—henry david thoreau

Contents

Preface   ix

Introduction   1

1 Experiencing Meaning   5

2 Standing Still   55

3 Stepping Aside   83

4 Stepping Back   111

5 Stepping on Someone Else   137

6 Stepping Up   163

Acknowledgments   191

Preface

When was the last time you made a decision that really mattered?

When I ask this question, people often pause before offering an answer. That's a healthy sign. I want you to pause and reflect on the way you make decisions. This book is intended to be a means for you to look inside yourself and to listen before you take actions so you can step up and make a difference by the decisions you make.

Included are over fifty inspirational stories of people who have stepped up throughout history. They represent the arts, business, religion, education, politics, sports, volunteerism, science, the trades, and many other working categories. Chapters include titles such as: Standing Still, Stepping Aside, Stepping Back, Stepping on Someone Else, and, of course, Stepping Up.

This book is far from inclusive of every subtle nuance on the decision-making process. For example, I don't say much about stepping out, stepping down, stepping away, stepping through, or even "stepping in it."

You will, however, bring your own opinions, history, and experiences to the five actions I do explore. That's what a book, especially this book, is supposed to do: invite you to enter, engage, begin to integrate new insights, and then return to the world more informed and inspired to make decisions that matter.

That way, when you reach the end of your journey you will be able to put the regrets aside and know you tried to step up as you make a difference in life and work. You will know you counted—that you matter. You will, I hope, be grateful for the life given you and the life you give to others by stepping up each and every day.

Timothy D. Dobbins
New York City
2006

STEPPING UP

Introduction

What do I say to his parents?

That's what I struggled with as I drove a borrowed car from an office in New York City down to Red Bank, New Jersey. I was heading to a memorial service for Lance Corporal Jourdan Grez, a twenty-four-year-old marine, killed in Iraq when his amphibious assault vehicle was struck by an improvised explosive device.

I was so distracted I almost forgot to change from one set of work clothes into the other. Pulling over at a rest stop along the Jersey Turnpike, I entered the facilities. Wriggling out of my jeans and sport shirt and into my suit, I tucked myself in, snapped on my clerical collar, and headed back down the highway, my transformation from business consultant to Episcopal priest complete. At least outwardly.

There was more than the Grez family tragedy on my mind that day. Years ago, while serving as a parish priest, I officiated at quite a few funerals and memorial services. So, like all clergy,

I've developed some elaborate inner defenses. But mine had been breached. My son was serving alongside Jourdan in Iraq. It could easily have been John's memorial service today.

The somber formality of the funeral home exterior snapped me out of my reverie and into the moment. I collected myself. As I entered the opulent interior and came face-to-face with Jourdan's casket and the gathered mourners, I realized what I needed to say. After spending a few private moments with the family, I rose to speak. I told everyone that I was representing the parents of the marines who couldn't attend, my son, and some of Jourdan's other buddies in Iraq. I also told them of the daunting question that had troubled me on my drive.

I said I knew if someone such as me, who has faced situations like this many times, was concerned about this, I was pretty sure most everyone else there was as well. Glancing over to Jourdan's family for their okay to begin, I suggested we all stop worrying about what to say, since that wasn't the most important thing. Our presence there said all that needed to be said, perhaps all that could be said. It also helped that Lance Corporal Grez's family conducted themselves with a grace and dignity that transcended the reality of the moment. It would have been easy for any of us to have avoided the gathering. No one would have thought less of us if we'd offered our condolences over the telephone, by letter, or even by e-mail. But we had all decided to step up and be there. I said it was our presence, not words said or left unsaid, that made a huge difference, not just to the family, not just to Jourdan, but to each other of us as well. After some further private moments and prayers with the family, I offered my condolences and headed back to New York.

To thank the friend who'd loaned me the car, I bought gas, drove it through a car wash, and then stopped at a liquor store to get a bottle of wine for him (and one for me). Explaining to the salesclerk that I was on my way back from a memorial service, I asked if I could use the store's bathroom to change. She readily agreed: sometimes a clerical collar has earthly advantages. Back in my corporate uniform I hopped into the car for my ride back to New York and retransformation. By the time I'd entered the elevator for the ride upstairs to one of my client's offices, my concerns had returned to the other work I love.

On the subway home that evening I let out an involuntary sigh and thought about what an exhausting and extraordinary day it had been. But as the train roared downtown, and I watched hundreds of people boarding and leaving the subway car at various stops, each secure in his or her own impenetrable urban bubble, I realized the day, while exhausting, wasn't extraordinary at all.

Every single day, each and every one of us has chance after chance to make a difference in the world, to step up.

It's obvious Lance Corporal Jourdan Grez stepped up and made a difference. He was doing his job. Whatever the merits of the war, Jourdan and his fellow marines, soldiers, sailors, and airmen and airwomen have all nobly volunteered to serve their nation. They chose to dedicate their lives for the duration of their enlistments to the service of their country and its citizens.

The mourners at Jourdan's memorial service had stepped up as well. They all could have found a reason to avoid such a painful event, sure to be filled with awkward moments and bound to provoke disquieting feelings. Yet they came to show their respect, support, and love for Jourdan and his family. In the simple act of being there they made a difference.

Every day, we are given opportunities to make a difference; chances to step up. Often these invitations are at work, where most of us spend most of our waking hours. They may come at home while you're sitting down with your family to breakfast. They could come in the office and involve a subordinate, superior, or customer. Or they might appear as you're walking down the street or riding the subway. Where they appear, when they occur, and what they involve doesn't matter. It's what you do when facing them that makes all the difference. Step up by making decisions in matters rare or regular, mundane or monumental, professional or personal, and you'll make a difference in the world and experience meaning in your life.

1

Experiencing Meaning

To exist is to change, to change is to mature, to mature is to go on creating oneself endlessly.

—Henri Bergson

I't's not just about the money.

You're good at what you do. You work long hours, and while you'd like to earn more, you may be earning a pretty good living. Perhaps you've acquired a certain amount of power, partly as a result of your skills and partly because you've learned how to climb the ladder and manage up. You care about your colleagues, your customers, and maybe even your business.

Despite all that, there are workdays when you feel you're just going through the motions, and others when you feel you're treading water, struggling just to keep from drowning in the minutiae of work and life. From the moment the alarm woke you in the morning to the minute your head hit the pillow at night, you were busy. You drank your morning coffee on the way to work, had lunch at your desk, and stayed late. Yet, as you close your eyes and try to think back on the day, you may not be able to single out anything you did that mattered. You may ask yourself, "Is this all there is?" String enough days like this together and soon you're feeling hollow. And string enough seemingly purposeless years together and you're convinced your work, and perhaps your life, is insignificant.

Well, you're not insignificant. Your work matters. Every day, in countless ways, you have an impact, not just in your work, but on the lives of your customers, clients, and coworkers. I know it may not seem that way. Being, say, marketing director of a breakfast-cereal company doesn't seem to be as meaningful as being a social worker or a teacher. But it can be. The seeds of making a difference are there all around you.

The emptiness you may be feeling inside is hunger; hunger to make a difference. Deep down you know work isn't just about money or power. Sure, you need to take care of yourself and provide for your family and future—we all do—but there's more to it than that. You need to feel that what you're doing counts; that your work and you matter. And you can feel that.

By stepping up—by making right, just, and loving decisions throughout your day—you'll experience meaning in your work and your life. You'll feel as if you're truly being the person you always thought you could be. You'll wake up in the morning maybe even wanting to go to work.

It costs so much to be a full human being that there are very few who have the enlightenment, or the courage, to pay the price. . . . One has to abandon altogether the search for security, and reach out to the risk of living with both arms. One has to embrace the world like a lover, and yet demand no easy return of love. One has to accept pain as a condition of existence. One has to court doubt and darkness as the cost of knowing. One needs a will stubborn in conflict, but apt always to the total acceptance of every consequence of living and dying.

—Morris L. West

THE EPIDEMIC OF EMPTINESS

You're not alone in feeling this hunger for meaning: emptiness is epidemic. I'm an Episcopal priest. Over the past twenty-five years I've ministered to hundreds of people who were facing death. Every one of them, whether it was the ninety-year-old family matriarch slowly drifting away or the nine-year-old boy losing his short and intense battle with cancer, asked me a similar question: "Did I matter? Have I counted? Did my life make a difference?" Since shifting my mission from parish work to the business world, I've seen how those questions don't just represent end-of-life personal doubts, but daily workplace uncertainties. You may not always frame it so directly or dramatically, but that emptiness you sometimes feel about your work comes from the fear that what you're doing doesn't really matter.

The epidemic of emptiness has even become part of popular culture. In the film *About Schmidt*, Jack Nicholson plays insurance executive Warren Schmidt, who retires and shortly thereafter loses his wife. The sudden changes force Schmidt to look back on his life, and he's not happy with what he sees: "I know we're all pretty small in the big scheme of things, and I suppose the most you can hope for is to make some kind of difference, but what kind of difference have I made? What in the world is better because of me?"

Perhaps this epidemic was spawned by all the graying baby boomers who are realizing that, despite years of dutifully paying into the corporate Holiday Club, they're unlikely to reach the bureaucratic heights to which they once aspired. Maybe it comes from our transition from an industrial to an information- and service-based economy: the more we're removed from the creation of a tangible product, the less "real," and therefore the less meaningful, our work seems. It could be that, as a society, we're undergoing a values shift away from materialism and consumption to spirituality and community. Maybe cynicism is waning and idealism is waxing. Who knows, it could even be the result of a great historical cycle linked to our entering a new millennium. While a discussion of the causes could be fascinating and is certainly worthy of a book, that's not what I'm writing about.

I entered the priesthood five years after graduating college and spent more than twenty years ministering to the needs of parishioners. I began at St. John's Episcopal Church Lafayette Square, known as the Church of the Presidents, right across from the White House in Washington, D.C. Next I went to St. John's Episcopal Church in the famed fishing town of Gloucester, Massachusetts. Finally, I served a well-heeled parish in a Philadelphia suburb.

Since leaving parish work, I've remained a priest but have worked as a communications specialist, conflict negotiator, and corporate consultant. I've often thought the Kris Kristofferson song "Pilgrim: Chapter 33" summed up my "career" pretty well: "He's a walkin' contradiction, partly truth and partly fiction / Takin' ev'ry wrong direction on his lonely way back home."

My own "lonely way back home" has led me to have a foot in both the spiritual and the business worlds. While I now spend most of my time in secular settings, I am in it, but not of it. This has provided me with the rare opportunity to see that the hunger for meaning is, as I suspected, just as common at work as it is in religious institutions. And I've found that you have far more chances to experience meaning and fill that emptiness at work than you may realize. That's certainly true for me: I often do more counseling in a day in the secular world than I did in a week as rector of a parish.

YOU HAVE LOTS OF CHANCES TO MAKE A DIFFERENCE

I know that might sound strange, but it's true. Most of us focus on our quest for meaning for perhaps ninety minutes or so a week. Maybe it's on Sunday morning when you attend church, on Saturday when you go to synagogue, or when you go to Friday-evening prayers at a mosque. It could be the ten minutes or so you spend meditating each day, or even your twenty-minute run after work. Whatever form our spirituality takes, we usually devote less time to it than to our daily commute. So while we may dedicate ourselves for those handful of minutes to our quest for meaning, by its nature it's a limited opportunity.

It's sort of like when the revival show comes to a town and the evangelist brings a quick fix of religion and faith to the crowd. Everyone comes to get their shot of "Jesus Juice" on Sunday morning, and it works for a day or two, and then by Tuesday the "saved ex-drinker" is back at the local bar. Or it's like the company that hires a motivational speaker to come in for a one-day seminar or a two-day "Cupcakes and Kumbaya" workshop to pump up morale, or the organization that provides yoga classes in response to employees' needs.

THE GOD BOX

I believe spirituality belongs not only in places of worship, but in the workplace as well. Spirituality is central to our full humanity. Since I'm an ordained clergyman, I'm sure that doesn't surprise you. But you might be surprised that I'm adamantly opposed to religion in the workplace. There's a big difference. God is how I choose to define the higher power I believe infuses all of us and all the universe. He/She can and does go by countless names ranging from ethereal spirit to scientific gravity. Spirituality is about the human spirit and soul; how each of us individually and collectively become conscious of ourselves and our unique roles in the universe. It's an expression of our values and beliefs. Religion, on the other hand, is a particular system of faith and belief with its own set of rules and practices.

To be the best managers, coworkers, employees, or just human beings that we can, we don't need to bring religion into the workplace, we just need to be mindful of our spiritual selves. We need to provide a space for our values and ethics to be expressed. We need to make room in the office or factory for the higher power. Ironically, at the same time we need to keep dogma out of the workplace. Diversity is a great strength, one that businesses need to embrace to succeed. Religion, by its very nature, can be exclusive rather than inclusive. Spirituality in the workplace can empower individuals, if its mystery is respected, and bring people together so we can all step up.

The answer to the hunger for meaning isn't a yoga class

during lunch hour or even an hour of prayer on the weekend. The answer is to experience meaning in your entire life, particularly at work, where you spend most of your time. Think of how much time you spend on the job. If you're like most of us, you're in the office for at least forty hours a week, and many of us are working a lot more than that, whether in the office, on the road, or at home. In an average day we may have a dozen different chances to make a difference. On the rush-hour drive to work we can allow someone to merge into our lane or we can force her to wait. On the way to our office we can ignore the man in the company cafeteria from whom we buy a cup of coffee or we can step up and smile and wish him a good day. When our superior asks about the status of a problematic project, we can step up and take responsibility or we can pass the buck. If our coworker is about to make a potential mistake, we can step up and intervene or we can just stay out of it. Those are four chances and we haven't even gotten to lunch yet.

Don't think smiling to the man who serves you coffee qualifies as making a difference? You're being an elitist. You see, making a difference isn't just about what you do, it's about how you do it. Sure, you could definitely make a difference by working as an elementary-school teacher in an inner-city school. But you could also make a difference by listening to the anger of a fellow department manager rather than striking back. The teacher educates a child and, let's say, instills a lifelong love of reading, making a tremendous difference in that child's life. The manager who chooses not to start internecine warfare in an organization not only stabilizes the environment but probably prevents financial turmoil that could lead to lower profits and possibly layoffs. Making a difference needn't be a dramatic direct action. You don't need to be like Alexander splitting the Gordian knot with his sword.

One of my clients, Gary Green, chief executive officer of Alliance Building Services, has told me that a manager's manner and the subtle setting of a tone can be like a pebble cast into a placid bay, sending out positive ripples that can turn into positive waves throughout an organization. He has focused on developing a "leadership of presence," where being is as important as doing. The success of his company is based on "the little things" as well as top-line growth. Your smile to the guy behind the coffee urn can turn into his exchanging pleasantries with the director of advertising, which results in her not blowing up at the staff meeting ten minutes later. Astronaut Neil Armstrong was making a profound statement when he first stepped onto the lunar surface and noted how what outwardly seems an almost insignificant act—a single human step—can have, pardon the pun, astronomical impact.

If your daily life seems poor, do not blame it; blame yourself that you are not poet enough to call forth its riches; for the Creator, there is no poverty.

—Rainer Maria Rilke

Just ask Chuck Henderson if little things make a difference.*The forty-seven-year-old married father of three is chief operating officer of a firm that produces components for high-tech electronic equipment. Short but well muscled with black, curly hair, Chuck's model for effective management is his college wrestling coach. One day he was struck by how down his payroll department manager seemed. The thirty-five-year-old woman had joined the firm six months earlier and had been doing a great job. When Chuck asked her what was wrong, she immediately launched into a series of apologies. Chuck reassured her and asked again. Finally, she explained that her husband had just started a new job as well, and their schedules kept them from spending as much time together as they'd like. She went on to note that they couldn't even take the same train into Manhattan from their suburban home, since she started work an hour earlier than he did. Chuck told me about the exchange later that afternoon during a meeting we were having on restructuring. Following our conversation and some reflection, he realized maybe flex hours could serve both the company and her marriage. Later that afternoon he went back to visit the payroll manager. He said he didn't see any reason why she couldn't just come into work one hour later and leave one hour later, so she could take the same train as her husband. It was as if he'd taken a ten-ton weight off her back. Her mo-

---

*I've changed the names of people and some of the details of the stories I use throughout this book to protect the privacy of my clients and parishioners. Rest assured that, while the details may have changed, the essential truths of the stories are unchanged.

rale soared and her productivity, already good, became exceptional. Simple solution; potent results.

Being mindful of our decisions

One reason why we don't experience all the chances we have to make a difference and find meaning at work is, we don't even think about the opportunities . . . we just react. Our boss expresses outrage at the press kits being late and we instinctively blame the vendor who we've used for years but "will never use again." One coworker dishes to us about a third coworker whose sales have fallen three quarters in a row and is about to be called on the carpet. We nod and take it all in just like always. A member of our project team shows up late again and explains he had to take his daughter to the doctor. We ask him not to let it happen again . . . even though it has become a regular occurrence and we've made the same request three times. Faced with situations at work, we fall into habitual, patterned behavior, just as we do in the rest of our lives. For better or worse, many of our decisions at work have become subconscious, like reflexes, rather than well-thought-out choices.

To step up and make a difference at work and, as a result, bring increased meaning to your life, you need to be mindful of the decisions you make during the day. You need to take responsibility for your actions. It's really all up to you. Meaning is there for you, but it won't come to you on its own, you have to reach out for it. God doesn't bestow a meaningful life on us, like a ripe apple falling off a tree into someone's lap. We're all given the gifts of free will and the opportunity to make a difference . . . if we so choose.

Doing work that matters comes not from the work itself, but from what you as an individual bring to it. You give meaning to the work; the work doesn't give meaning to you. That's as true for a social worker helping to feed the hungry as it is for the chief financial officer of a construction supply company. If the social worker doesn't step up, his work at the soup kitchen won't feel meaningful. And if the chief financial officer does step up, her work for the annual report can have real meaning.

Sharon Campbell, sixty-one, has been a human resources professional for more than thirty years. A divorced woman with stylish, shoulder-length gray hair, Sharon was educated in both social work and management. She went into human resources fully intending to do all she could to bring a therapeutic touch to the corporate world. You'd think she was perfectly situated to find her work meaningful. But today, working in the HR department of a major financial company, she finds herself spending nine hours a day filling out government compliance forms and working on termination packages. Sharon has confided to me that she has actually started counting the days until retirement.

Winston Cliff, fifty-nine, works as a security guard for the same financial company where Sharon works. His job is to manage the flow of who can enter the building. If you were going to pick a job that made a difference, you wouldn't pick his. Yet you'd be wrong. A married father of four, Winston has the build of an NFL offensive lineman. He has a shaved head and wears a perpetual smile. No one, from corporate executives to the deliveryman dropping off a pastrami sandwich, or at best an occasional visitor to the company, enters the building without a kind word, a shared joke, or a pat on the back. Winston's stepping up in his interactions with others casts a glow on the whole company for employees and visitors alike.*

Your options

To step up and bring meaning to your work life you need to go through the day mindfully. That means thinking rather than just reacting to situations. Every day you face a number of different choices requiring you to make decisions that will result in consequences for you, for others, and for people with whom you work. That's one of the mantras I'm always reinforcing with my clients: choices, decisions, consequences. Stepping up requires looking at the options you have and trying to decide what is the just and loving thing to do, not just looking for the easiest or most typical response. That doesn't mean you'll always choose the "softest" option. Sometimes stepping up can be tough and hard work for everyone.

I think you can divide humanity into three types of people: people who watch things happen, people who make things happen, and people who wonder what happened. Stepping up

---

*Ironically, Winston was once fired for being too friendly with people. Some bean counter in the company decided he was costing the company money because people spent too much time chatting with him. Thankfully, a number of executives in the company stepped up and spoke with the bean counter. Winston was back at his post the next day.

means consciously becoming one of those people who make things happen.

STEPPING UP TO HELP THE NEEDY

George Frideric Handel's career was on a downward spiral. For more than thirty years he had been both a popular and critical star, but in the summer of 1741 those days seemed long gone. The fifty-six-year-old composer was plagued by depression, suffered from rheumatism, and feared he'd end his days in a debtors' prison. Then he received two letters.

The first was an invitation from the Duke of Devonshire to come to Dublin and produce a series of benefit concerts for the poor who were imprisoned or hospitalized. Handel decided to step up and accept the invitation. Then a second letter arrived from a former collaborator, Charles Jennens, containing some new lyrics drawn from biblical verses.

Handel could have viewed the commission as a way to quickly earn some much needed cash. Or he could have done what he knew others expected and produce a conventional composition. Instead he stepped up.

Moved by the lyrics and inspired by the idea of helping the poor, Handel locked himself in his study for three weeks and composed the *Messiah*. At the premiere King George II was so moved during the "Hallelujah Chorus" that he stood, feeling not even an earthly monarch should remain seated in God's presence. In response the entire audience rose to its feet, starting a tradition that remains to this day. Stepping up (and standing up) to the challenge, Handel not only resurrected his career and finances, but, in the words of the historian Charles Burney, "fed the hungry, clothed the naked, and fostered the orphan."

The situation could involve something happening to us, such as the chairman telling you the board has decided to create a new executive vice president position whose responsibilities sound remarkably like some of your own. It could also be something happening to a coworker or customer, say you hear a rumor that one of your coworkers has developed a drinking problem. Or it could be something happening to the company, such as a customer whose business is threatened by a new product you learn is about to be released by a competitor. In each of those situations, and in every other situation, there are at least five paths you can follow, five choices you can make:

- You can stand still and do nothing;

- You can step aside and avoid taking action, forcing or allowing someone else to do it;

- You can step back and block others from taking necessary action;

- You can take advantage of the situation and step on someone to take revenge or improve your position; or

- You can step up and do the right thing.

When you step up and do the right thing, the loving thing, you help other people, help your company, help your community, help your family, and help yourself by experiencing greater meaning in your life.

What should you do?

Let's look at a hypothetical workplace scenario and see how each of the five options look in the real world. Say you're part of the sales team at a high-end consumer electronics store. Four of you work the sales floor, and you all report to the store's sales manager. The company announces a $1,000 bonus to the salesperson who generates the most revenue over the next four weeks, which make up the holiday selling season. All four of you have performed about evenly all year long, so the bonus is really up for grabs. Besides you, there's Melissa, a young woman in her twenties who married just a year ago; Steve, an aggressive salesman in his midthirties who's looking to get a job selling for a consumer electronics manufacturer; and Eva, a longtime employee in her forties who'd like to become the next store manager.

After the first week of the competition you notice that Melissa is working at a feverish pace. She's pouncing on customers as they walk in the door, refusing to take breaks for lunch or dinner, and working twelve-hour days, seven days a week. Late the next Monday afternoon you are chatting with Steve and Eva at the coffee machine when you all notice an exhausted Melissa drag herself into the bathroom. She's in there for a couple of minutes and then emerges as if she were shot out of a cannon. You offhandedly ask, "What's up with her?" Steve smirks, then rather than saying anything closes one of his nostrils with a knuckle and makes a snorting sound. "I can't believe she's going to win the bonus by getting coked up," he says before going back out onto the sales floor. Eva shakes her head from side to side. "I actually feel bad for her," she adds. "I hear her husband is out of work and they're pretty desperate. Maybe you should talk to the boss about getting her help." You don't respond. Eva leaves the room. You're faced with a decision.

You could stand still and do nothing. Maybe Melissa will win the bonus, aided by her drug problem. Maybe Steve will complain to the boss and get her fired. Maybe Eva will talk to the boss about getting her help. Or maybe nothing will happen. Whatever the case, the easiest thing is to not get involved.

You could step aside and actively avoid taking action. You can go to Eva and tell her that you don't want to get involved. If she'd like to talk to the boss, that's fine, but you're not going to be part of it.

You could step back and block others from taking action. You can go to Eva and talk her out of speaking to the boss, saying that could result in Melissa getting fired, or in Eva's own future being jeopardized.

You could take advantage of the situation by stepping on someone. You can go to the boss yourself, explain that Melissa has been bringing illegal drugs into the store, and perhaps improve your own situation, not just at her expense, but at Steve's and Eva's expense as well.

Or you could step up and do the right thing. You can ask Steve and Eva to join with you and all three go to Melissa together and tell her you know what's going on. You could tell her that none of you want to go to the boss, but that you all need her to take responsibility and to get help for her problem.

Let's take a more in-depth look at each of the five options.

STEPPING UP FOR THE UNRECOGNIZED

Ted Williams is thought by many to be the greatest hitter in baseball history. An irascible perfectionist, Williams had a love/hate relationship with the fans and press of Boston during his long career with the Red Sox. But throughout his life he stepped up off the field as well as on. When the Korean War broke out, Williams left baseball during what would have been his prime years, to fly a fighter in combat for the U.S. Marine Corps. But just as dramatic was how he stepped up during his induction into the Baseball Hall of Fame on July 25, 1966, in Cooperstown, New York.

Williams thanked the usual people, but then became the first inductee to speak the unspeakable: "The other day Willie Mays hit his five hundred and twenty-second home run. He has gone past me, and he's pushing, and I say to him, 'Go get 'em, Willie.' Baseball gives every American boy a chance to excel. Not just to be as good as anybody else, but to be better. This is the nature of man and the name of the game. I hope someday Satchel Paige and Josh Gibson will be voted into the Hall of Fame as symbols of the great Negro players who are not here only because they weren't given the chance." Five years later, in 1971 Satchel Paige became the first Negro League player inducted into the Hall of Fame. He was followed the next year by Josh Gibson.

Standing still

Standing still is the default option for almost all of us. To stand still is to let something happen without taking any action. Things might work out, or they might not, but in either case your action is inaction. Your motivation might be self-preservation, fear of failure, opportunism, jealousy, or simple laziness. I think this is our default option since we've all been brought up to believe that it's better to do nothing than to do something wrong. So if we have any qualms or concerns—and who doesn't—we simply stand still. You may tell yourself you're being proactive, or perhaps that you're being neutral. But actually you're ignoring your responsibility. To paraphrase a verse from the book of Genesis: you are your coworker's and customer's keeper. You're also your own keeper.

One common way we stand still is by subtly shifting the responsibility for making a decision onto someone else. We do that by asking someone for permission to take an action we, deep down, know is the loving thing to do.

Let's say one Saturday morning you get a telephone call from your aging mother, asking you to come over to her apartment that afternoon to help her fill out her taxes, which she has left to the last minute. Your first response might be to talk to your partner and ask if he would mind if you run over to your mother's place. That's what you've always done in similar situations in the past. And the dialogue will probably follow a familiar pattern. Your partner, never a big fan of your mother for a variety of reasons, will be angry that you're giving up a Saturday that you could have spent with him. Consciously or subconsciously, he'll make you feel bad for wanting to help

your mother. That, in turn, will make you angry. You'll probably end up going over to your mother's anyway, but with both
you and your partner in a bad mood.

I believe it's often better to ask for forgiveness than permission. Rather than standing still and shifting the responsibility
for your decision onto your partner, step up, go to your
mother's, and then, afterward, ask your partner for forgiveness
if he is angry at your actions. Whenever you feel yourself about
to ask for permission, you should ask yourself, what is the
worst thing that could happen? Can it be overcome? If you go
to your mother's, the worst thing that could happen is your
partner will be angry at you for a brief time. But if you ask for
permission instead, he'll probably be angry at you for just con-
sidering the option. If you just do it and ask for forgiveness
afterward, you'll be stepping up for your mother and for yourself. Stepping up isn't about who's right and who's wrong; it's
about what's right and what's wrong.

You'd be standing still if, when you learn of the appointment of the new executive vice president, you don't ask the
chairman why the position was created or how the board sees
you interacting with the new person. You don't help the new
appointee, but neither do you hinder her. You might tell yourself you're just biding your time, but actually you're frozen with
fear. You'd also be standing still if, when you hear the rumor
about your coworker's alcohol addiction, you instinctively shut
down. You don't tell the rumormonger to stop telling tales out
of school, you don't warn or try to counsel your coworker, and
you don't use the information to stab your coworker in the
back. You stand still and watch things happen. Standing still
when you hear of a new product introduction that could hurt

your customer means you don't warn him, don't bring the possibly strategic information to your superiors, and don't actively try to switch allegiance to your customer's competitor. You stand still and watch the train wreck take place.

STEPPING UP BY DISOBEYING ORDERS

There are many stories surrounding the terrible massacre of the Macdonalds of Glencoe in 1692. One of the most moving is about an English soldier in the regiment responsible for the massacre of the Scottish clan.

During the horrible event an officer learns about a woman and child who have escaped the slaughter and are hiding under a bridge. The officer takes a patrol out to search for the survivors. While out on patrol they hear a child's cry. The officer sends the soldier out to kill the woman and child. The soldier finds the woman and her baby hiding with their loyal dog. The soldier takes pity on the two and decides he'll kill the dog and show the blood on his bayonet to his officer as "proof" he's killed the woman and child. But when he shows his proof, his officer whips him with his cane. "That's not human blood," the officer barks. "Kill the woman and child or I'll kill you and have someone else do the killing anyway." The soldier went back to the hiding place. He had the mother gag the child with her plaid to stifle its cries. Then he cut off the child's little finger and smeared the blood on his bayonet. That was all the proof the officer needed to satiate his bloodlust.

Years later the soldier, now an old wanderer, is staying in a Highland inn. Over a drink at night he's asked what was the most terrible thing he'd ever seen, and he answers, the massacre at Glencoe.

That night, the innkeeper decides he'll kill the old soldier in the morning as revenge for the crime. Over breakfast the next day the old soldier is asked to tell the story of Glencoe and describes his encounter with the woman and her child. When he finishes his story, the innkeeper holds up a hand. Its little finger is missing. The old soldier and the innkeeper embrace.

Monica Van Dorn, forty-four, was watching a train wreck . . . and she was driving the locomotive. A charming if somewhat staid woman with straight black hair she usually wears pulled back, Monica is an assistant vice president of a midsize insurance company. I was working at the company for a couple of months helping them integrate a recent acquisition. When Monica came in to see me, the first thing she said was "I need a divorce." I instinctively started to shift into pastoral mode, but she quickly added, with a chuckle, "I've been working under Don Hagel for nineteen years and I've got to split from him." Monica probably knows more and is more skilled than most of the other vice presidents in the company. But her immediate superior has been, unconsciously I believe, holding her back from being all she could be. Monica bears some responsibility as well, since whenever she has had a chance to step up and break free from Don, either inside the company or by taking another job, she has reflexively gone to him to ask permission. And Don, determined to keep her on board and under his control, has never given it. As a result, Monica has been standing still for nearly two decades.

Stepping aside

If standing still is ignoring your responsibility, stepping aside can be an abdication. It's taking yourself out of the game, giving up, waving a white flag, and telling someone else to take your place. We give up in workplace situations for the same reasons we give up in any other arena of life. Maybe you feel you're destined to lose, so rather than suffer battle damage you decide to surrender and save yourself more pain. You might feel someone breathing down your neck, let's say, in a competition to head up a new project team, and rather than stepping up and taking leadership responsibility you step aside and let someone else take the reins. It could be you honestly think someone else is better than you, and so you step aside and let her lead the charge. Whether that's due to a poor self-image or a practical appreciation of your own shortcomings doesn't matter. In either case you've passed the baton to someone else and have relegated yourself to the background. Perhaps you think the situation is so potentially dangerous you'd rather maneuver so someone else does the hard work, after which you'll be better positioned to move ahead. Or it could be you're looking to help someone else and honestly believe letting her take your place would be "a good deed."

You'd be stepping aside if, when you learn of the appointment of the new executive vice president, you tell the chairman you're relieved someone else will be taking over those responsibilities so you can concentrate on what you do best. In effect you're endorsing the reasons for creating the new position, without knowing what those reasons were. You'd also be stepping aside if, when you hear the rumor about your coworker's alcoholism, instead of doing something youself, you encourage the gossiper to deal with the problem by speaking with the alleged addict or using the information. Rather than involving yourself you leave it to someone else to respond. How do you step aside when you hear of a new product introduction that could hurt your customer? You leave it to others to pass along the news or investigate the ramifications for your own company.

STEPPING UP BY SETTING PRIORITIES

Sam Rayburn of Texas was perhaps the most powerful Speaker of the House in American history, but he seems never to have forgotten what mattered in life. The daughter of a newspaper reporter with whom Rayburn was friendly died suddenly. The next morning there was a knock on the door of the newspaper reporter's apartment. When the reporter answered the door, he saw it was Speaker Rayburn. "I just came by to see what I could do to help," the Speaker said. The reporter, stunned by the visit, said he didn't think there was anything the Speaker could do. "Have you had your coffee yet this morning?" Rayburn asked. When the reporter admitted that he hadn't, the Speaker said he'd make the coffee. While the reporter was getting some papers together, he suddenly remembered something. He went into the kitchen, where he found Rayburn turning on the coffee. The reporter said that he'd just remembered the Speaker was supposed to have breakfast at the White House that morning. Rayburn admitted that was true. "But I called the president and told him I had a friend who was in trouble, and I couldn't come."

A few years ago I was at a meeting of a not-for-profit organization on whose board I sit. The organization decided on the need for a diversity initiative. Because I've been a part of efforts to bring people of different backgrounds together since my teenage years—as president of my high school class in Florida I helped integrate the school—I was asked to head up the task force. I was touched by the suggestion, but I was also worried. I had just lined up a couple of major new corporate clients, which would be taking up a lot of my time. I'd signed a contract to write this book. My older son, a marine reservist, would soon be heading to Iraq. My younger son was preparing to graduate high school and head off to college. I didn't think I needed anything else on my table right then.

Also sitting on the board of the organization is Jerome Taylor, a thirty-nine-year-old African American entrepreneur who had recently made a great deal of money by selling his company to a multinational corporation. Jerome was just starting to get involved in "giving back" to his community. I told myself that it would be a great thing for Jerome to head up the task force. Not only was it dealing with an issue close to his heart, but it would give him a chance to "step up." So, I stepped aside and successfully advocated for Jerome to take the lead. He did, but unfortunately with his entrepreneurial streak he didn't mesh well with the others on the task force, most of whom were used to consensus building. The task force was unsuccessful. Deep down I knew I was the right person to lead the effort, but I had stepped aside, rationalizing it by telling myself I was really stepping up.

Stepping back

We step back to block others from moving forward. Often workplace stepping back takes place in team or group projects. Consciously or unconsciously you block the team or group from moving in a direction that may not meet your own needs. It's often motivated by a fear that someone else, probably someone in the group, is somehow usurping you. If standing still is passive indecision, stepping back is active indecision; it's sabotage so no one else can take responsibility. Think of it as putting up roadblocks, whether real or imagined.

STEPPING UP BY BREAKING THE LAW

Some scientists in late 1930s' Germany could sense what the future might hold for them if they didn't flee. Nobel laureates James Franck and Max von Laue were worried, not just about themselves and their families, but about what they should do with their gold Nobel medals. Neither wanted the gold to go to Hitler's regime, but they knew it was a capital crime to send gold out of the country. They decided to smuggle their medals to Denmark, where they could be safeguarded by their friend and fellow Nobel laureate Niels Bohr.

Not long after war broke out, Denmark too was threatened with invasion. Bohr went to his friend and chemist Georg von Hevesy and told him about the medals. Still not wanting the medals to fall into Hitler's hands, but fearful that if they were found they'd result in the deaths of the two German scientists, they knew they had to come up with a foolproof way to hide them. They decided to step up by dissolving the medals in a mixture of hydrochloric and nitric acids. With German troops literally marching down the streets of Copenhagen, Hevesy and Bohr melted their friends' medals and kept the solution in a jar on the shelf of Bohr's laboratory. In a few months Bohr himself escaped Denmark and fled to England, taking his own medal with him but leaving the inconspicuous jar on his lab shelf.

When the war ended and Bohr returned home, he found the jar still sitting safely on the shelf. The gold was recovered from the solution, and the Nobel Foundation recast it into two commemorative medals for Franck and von Laue.

Since this is a path often taken in group situations, let's change our examples just a bit. Instead of your learning of the creation of a new executive vice president position that infringes on some of your responsibility, let's say you're part of a committee with the task of writing the job description for a new executive vice president position. Stepping back would involve your throwing up roadblocks whenever you perceive any of your turf is threatened, even if the committee seems agreed everyone needs to give up a bit to make the reorganization work. Instead of your learning about a coworker's rumored addiction in a whispered exchange at the watercooler, let's say you're part of a team formed to launch a new product line. You'd be stepping back if you used the information of another team member's rumored addiction as a way to block adoption of her plan rather than your own. Instead of learning that a customer is threatened by a new product introduction, let's say you've been in an ongoing set of meetings to decide which customers should get priority in the coming year. You'd be stepping back if you withheld the information in order to keep the group from lowering the priority of your own customer.

Peter Greenberg, fifty-seven, is head of research and development for a midsize firm that manufactures small printers for applications such as gas pumps and cash registers. A tall, thin, intense fellow with thinning brown hair and a closely cropped beard, Peter's strength is his engineering background. I was brought into the company to help the CEO, Jeremy Smith, redefine strategic goals, including the development of a leadership team that could help set key performance indicators. Peter was part of the leadership team, as were the heads of sales and finance. During a strategic retreat for the leadership team, Peter fell into the role of naysayer. I learned from Jeremy that Peter and Larry, the head of sales, were viewed as the two leading candidates to succeed Jeremy as CEO. They represented the two factions—sales versus engineering—that had long vied for control of the organization. Peter was actively trying to block every opportunity for his rival to contribute to the company's success. He wasn't bad-mouthing the head of sales personally. He was instead pointing out the potential downsides to every suggestion or idea his rival offered. Rather than stepping up to improve the organization by offering ways to make his rival's ideas workable, or by advocating for his own forward-looking agenda, Peter was stepping back to block his perceived rival from succeeding.

GIVING GOOD MEETING

You don't have to be trying to step back in order to destroy a meeting. Many if not most business meetings are disasters. I tell my clients that any time more than two people get together, five things can happen:

- They can gather and give information;

- They can receive feedback;

- They can solve problems;

- They can do team building; and/or

- They can make decisions.

Since running a good meeting is a core competency for corporate success, it's important for a leader to tell the people before and at the meeting which of these five things are the object of the gathering. This prevents subagendums from taking priority or others from hijacking the meeting. The fewer of these goals you set for each meeting, the more efficient and effective it will be. In addition, by keeping the meeting focused on just one or two of the goals, you show your recognition of the complexity of the process.

Stepping on someone

Business is almost always portrayed as a zero-sum game: for one party to win, the other must lose. While that may be true for most (but not all) of the interactions between individual companies and organizations, I don't believe it's true of most of the interactions between individuals within companies and organizations. Just because your company's goal is to take market share away from your competitors, that doesn't mean your personal goal needs to be to take responsibilities and power away from your coworkers. I know some organizations have cultures that promote that kind of environment. I take that back: I know lots of organizations that encourage civil war. But having worked in the corporate world, and having worked as a conflict negotiator, I also know it doesn't have to be that way. By stepping up you can lead the change in your own corporate culture.

Stepping on someone means eliminating someone or something that stands in your way. Let's go back to our original examples. You'd be stepping on someone if, when you learn of the appointment of the new executive vice president, you tell the chairman you've learned some damaging information about the prime candidate. Or, if you don't immediately have the name and info at hand, you bide your time and then do everything in your power to destroy the individual in order to preserve your power. You'd also be stepping on someone if, when you hear the rumor about your coworker's drinking, you either spread the information around the company, bring the rumor to your mutual superior, or get word back to her family, all in an effort to destroy your coworker so she's not a threat to your advancement. Stepping on someone would mean that when you hear of a new product introduction that could hurt your customer, you take all your inside knowledge of their operations and use it to ingratiate yourself with the company that's threatening your current customer.

While stepping on someone seems to be an overt and conscious act, I've found that's not always the case. At times when people perceive some kind of slight or betrayal, rather than stepping up and discussing their feelings openly, they attack the other person by stepping on them. That was the case with Terry Smith. A forty-three-year-old programming executive at a cable television channel, Terry is an athletic-looking young man with closely cropped blond hair, whose workplace uniform is blue jeans, blazer, and an open-neck tennis shirt. One of Terry's first acts when he joined the network was to hire a programming consultant. Sherri Morgan, also forty-three, had worked with Terry on and off for a number of years back when they both worked in network television. Always an astute reader of the zeitgeist, Sherri had struck out on her own as a consultant. With her help, Terry was able to increase ratings and advertising revenue at his cable channel. Soon, programming executives at other channels owned by the same parent network as Terry's channel were asking him if they could hire Sherri to help them develop their own new programming. Terry, angry that Sherri was getting some kudos that could have gone to him, and hurt that Sherri would be willing to work for others, stepped on her, rather than stepping up. In a number of casual conversations he damned her with faint praise and insinuated that she might have overcharged for her services. Rather than stepping up to help his colleagues and his friend, he guaranteed Sherri wouldn't get further clients at the network.

STEPPING UP BY CREATING DIALOGUES

When my father retired in the late 1960s, our family finally settled down in Gainesville, Florida. Back then the schools in Alachua County were segregated, so the high school I was attending was almost entirely white. Then, in 1969, a federal judge ordered the integration of the school system. The African American high school, Lincoln High, was closed, and the twelve hundred students there were transferred to join the twenty-five hundred students at Gainesville High.

It was not a smooth transition. Carloads of agitators, from the KKK as well as the Black Panthers, came down from Alabama and Georgia to try to stir things up. They succeeded. For a couple of years there were riots and fights almost every week. In the midst of all this I decided to run for student body president. Because I was one of the few people who could actually communicate and get along with both "camps," I ended up being elected for the years 1971 and 1972. I made it my mission to create dialogues among students to find ways for everyone to air their differences constructively rather than yell at each other and fight. The principal, Dan Boyd, was capable of being both authority figure and friend. He was not only my great support but we were also a team.

Looking back, I understand why I stepped up. I'd moved nine times by the age of fifteen, and Gainesville was the first place that had ever felt like home. This was the sense of community I'd been seeking my whole life. I couldn't just step aside and watch it shatter. Sure, I was motivated to work at my studies, but I was looking for something more than just good grades. I wanted to do something that mattered, that was meaningful. I wanted to step up.

I know that sometimes the desire to step on someone who has previously been abusive and hurtful can be overwhelming. Confronted with an opportunity to take revenge, to balance the scales, to seek vengeance, we may grab the chance and step on someone who has done wrong. Payback may actually be rewarding in the short term. Getting even with someone who's done wrong to you or others can be immediately satisfying. You'll feel as if the universe is somehow back in balance; that justice has triumphed, that right and good have won out in the end. But the victory is fleeting.

Your stepping on people who have stepped on you in the past will, in the long run, perpetuate their poor behavior. By adopting the same tactics as them, whatever your motivation, you endorse their actions. They'll come away from the situation feeling that stepping on someone else is okay . . . they just need to step harder. The way to stop the behavior forever is to demonstrate that there's a better choice; that they could step up instead.

Stepping up

I truly believe that, on some level, we almost always know what the right thing to do is in any situation. I don't know if it's a God-given gift, genetic programming, or part of being socialized. I just know the answer is almost always there, somewhere inside. I'm not saying we have all the right words and the exact tactics already inside us, just waiting to be called up when the time comes. And sure, at times situations are so complex that the right path requires a great deal of thought. But in most situations we have a general sense of what should be done, or what needs to be done. I think, if you give yourself a chance, you'll know what you need to do to step up. (Obviously, the "right thing" for one person can be the "wrong thing" for another. More on this later.)

Stepping up is all about doing the true, just, and loving thing. It's about choosing to do what's best for the other person, for the company, and, yes, for yourself too. I don't think those are competing goals. You see, by doing what's best for the company, or what's best for your coworkers, you help yourself too. By stepping up you will bring meaning to your work and your life. Do the right thing at work and you will feel better about yourself and your life. Step up and you'll never wonder if you made a difference. You'll know you did.

So why don't we always step up if the results are so beneficial? I think part of it is that we spend much of our lives seeing ourselves as we think others see us. Too often our self-image comes not from deep inside us, but from outside. That leads us to take actions consistent with what we think is expected, what is conventional, even if in our gut we know we should act differently. We do things not because we think we should, but because we think everyone else thinks we should. The first four actions—standing still, stepping aside, stepping back, and stepping on someone—are more often than not unconscious, reflexive choices. For instance, in a business environment that encourages and rewards stepping on people, you might choose

KEEP YOUR EYE ON THE RABBIT

A world-famous journalist found herself getting cynical and jaded about almost everything. One day she heard about an incredibly wise man who was living in a remote region of Central Asia. Having vacation time saved up, sensing her own need to go on some kind of quest, and thinking it might even turn into a great story, she decided to find the reclusive wise man.

She spent weeks chasing down leads and following up tips. Finally, after a three-day trek she found the wise man for whom she'd been searching. A bald, shriveled figure, he was squatting on the ground outside a yurt on the edge of a primitive village, his dog lying at his side. Slowly but surely, the journalist began asking the wise man questions, trying in her practiced manner to work her way up to the vital questions and answers about the meaning of life.

In the midst of her questioning, she saw the wise man's dog spring to his feet. In the next split second she saw all the other dogs in the village spring to their feet as well. Suddenly, the wise man's dog began running into the fields chasing a rabbit he'd spied. Amidst a chorus of barks and growls all the other dogs in the village joined the chase. Distracted, the journalist tried to get back on track and ask her questions. But out of the corner of her eye she saw the dogs, one by one, return to the village. Soon, only the wise man's dog was missing.

Then, a few minutes later, the wise man's dog came trotting back with a rabbit in his mouth. Unable to resist, the journalist asked the wise man why his dog was the only one to persist in the chase. The wise man laughed. "Finally, a good question," he chortled. "My dog was chasing the rabbit. The other dogs never saw the rabbit, they were chasing my dog and the commotion."

that option, not because you're bad or you don't know any better, but because it's the expected choice.

Stepping up is the hardest to follow of the five choices; it takes the most effort. It can require breaking out of behavioral patterns and going against organizational norms. It's making the aware and helpful choice. The truth is that if you can make the leap of faith and step up—despite its taking more effort, and even though it flies in the face of what's expected—you will be changing things. Step up and you'll be making it easier for others to step up later on. Step up and you'll be improving the culture of your workplace. Step up and you'll be building an environment in which others can live a conscious, creative life. Step up and you'll be making a difference. Step up and you won't end up like Warren Schmidt in the movie *About Schmidt*.

At the end of the film, Schmidt reveals himself in a letter to the only person with whom he feels he can communicate frankly—a six-year-old Tanzanian boy named Ndugu he has "adopted" through a children's charity. "Relatively soon, I will die," he writes. "Maybe in twenty years, maybe tomorrow, it doesn't matter. Once I am dead and everyone who knew me dies too, it will be as though I never existed. What difference has my life made to anyone? None that I can think of. None at all."

Through the following chapters I'll be focusing on the choices we make in our personal and work lives. I'll be writing about how if we don't step up, we're falling short of being all that we could be for ourselves and others, of experiencing meaning in our lives. But things aren't really that simple. Stepping up isn't just doing something; it's being aware or awake to what we're capable of doing and being. To step up means to make a conscious rather than reflexive or instinctive choice. It means pausing—whether for a moment's thought or a few days of reflection—before you make a decision. As I'll show throughout this book, it's even possible to step up by standing still, to step up by stepping aside, to step up by stepping back, and even to step up by stepping on someone else. Stepping up is doing the right deed, whatever that may be.

Don't get lost in the numbers

Derek Wilkes did the right thing for the right reason. Derek was a bundle of nervous energy when I first met him. A born salesman who had never been to college, he'd been peddling records in one way or another for forty of his fifty years. A rotund, rumpled man with a cockney accent, he'd been raised in London's East End by his widowed father, who peddled the *Evening Standard* newspaper on the streets. Derek had called me to help him integrate the sales staffs of five different music labels, all of which had been brought together by one parent company. Derek had headed up sales for one of the labels and now had only a short time to unify what had been five highly competitive teams. He started our meeting by calling for the organization charts of each sales staff. Then he printed out past sales reports and future projections for each team. With all the paper spread out on the floor of his office, Derek got down on his knees and began making piles and shuffling them around in an ever-changing pattern. I put a hand on his shoulder to stop him. I said I knew he hadn't brought me in to help him organize paper. Then I looked at him and asked, "Derek, what do you want? What do you really want?"

Derek could have come up with a conventional answer. He could have told me he wanted to cut the staff in half to reduce costs, or to increase sales by 10 percent per year. But he took a moment to think and then stepped up. He said, "I love to come to the office every day. I want my people to wake up wanting to come to work." I said, in that case, that goal should drive every decision he made from here on. Some people had to be let go, but Derek ended up doing it in a humane way that served everyone, not just the bottom line. He made sure the company provided outplacement counseling and personally tapped into his own network to help find positions for those who had to be fired. Derek set up an office suite, with equipment and support staff, for the use of those who were being let go. Severance packages were maximized and benefits were continued as long as possible. The care and humanity he showed those who were let go had an effect, not just on them, but on those who remained. The result was an enthusiastic and efficient sales organization that generated higher sales. Word spread throughout the industry that this was a company that cared about its sales staff.

Just keep on leading

Ramon Salazar was having that same kind of success in his business. In only four years, Ramon, thirty-eight, had turned a small trade newsletter into a "must read" in his industry. The impeccably-dressed, dark-haired young man had taken what others had seen as a dead-end assignment after working for the parent trade-magazine company for only a year. Ramon saw it as a niche he could make his own. And he did just that. Hiring a small staff of young, eager reporters, he built incredible team spirit by providing flexible schedules and an informal work environment. At times other departments heading home would pass some of Ramon's staff who were just coming in, prepared to pull an all-nighter to nail down a story from the Far East. And they'd be followed by Ramon carrying a stack of pizzas for them. The success of Ramon's newsletter was one reason a major international publishing firm decided to acquire his parent company. The new owner has a reputation for being conservative about both financial and organizational matters.

I'm a friend of Ramon's mother. When she heard of his situation, she suggested he give me a call since I have experience with mergers and acquisitions. Ramon filled me in on his situation during an hour-long meeting. Toward the end of the conversation, Ramon and I went over his options. He could rein in his staff, in effect lowering the newsletter's profile, so as not to become a target. He could look to change his style to match what he believed was the new owner's approach. Or he could just keep on doing what he was doing. Ramon could have pursued one of the safer, more conventional options, as most of the other department heads seemed to be doing. Instead he stepped up and kept on leading his staff as he had before, earning even more respect, loyalty, and effort from his team.

BEWARE MANAGERS BEARING GIFTS

I'm often called on to coach executives who are dealing with a newly merged organization. One of the things I tell them is to beware the manager or department head who "sends the first flowers" or who is most effusive in his or her expressions of welcome. He or she is the one most likely to play power politics and cause problems later on. The manager or department head who hides, while not a threat, isn't an ally either. He or she is in self-preservation mode and won't want to commit to any kind of change. Your true allies, I tell them, are likely to come from among the managers or department heads who just keep on doing what they were doing before. This word of caution extends to those who are internally promoted as well.

Stay in the game

Debbie Siragusa had the trauma of seeing her personal support "team" vanish. Debbie, forty-three, brings a warmth to any room she enters. A bright-eyed woman with a ready smile and shoulder-length, wavy brown hair, Debbie has been a successful professional recruiter for more than a decade. Yet in just six months she saw much of her life's foundation crumble. It began with the untimely death of her husband, Roger, a college professor, in an auto accident. Debbie was left a great deal of money, but was still the sole parent of their two young sons, one of whom has a learning disability. Debbie's childhood friend Angela, who had been a huge help to Debbie in dealing with Roger's death, was diagnosed with ovarian cancer and died shortly thereafter. In the midst of all this personal trauma, Debbie learned one of her partners in the recruiting business was leaving, forcing her to shoulder a heavier load at work. Debbie felt as if she were under siege from life.

Debbie could easily have given up. I think most of us would. She had enough money in the bank to stop working, at least for a while. But she didn't. She stepped up by taking a deep breath and diving back into work. She accepted the challenges life threw at her and took responsibility for her company, her employees, her children, and herself. The juggling is difficult, but she knows she's making a difference.

Dealing with a pain in the neck

I know how tempted Debbie must have felt to give in to her pain and shut down. When you have a run of misfortune, it feels as if the bad times will never end. From 1995 through 1997 I had terrible physical problems. It began with rotator-cuff surgery on my right shoulder. A childhood filled with baseball and an adulthood filled with tennis and squash were capped by having my shoulder being slammed in a closing gate. While I was recovering from the shoulder surgery, I suffered from the first of what would become a series of six kidney stones. Feeling as if the bad times had finally passed, I took my two sons to an amusement park for the day. While riding on a roller coaster with them, I felt my neck snap. I thought I'd pulled a muscle, but when the pain kept getting worse rather than going away, I went to my doctor. An X-ray revealed I had a cracked vertebra in my neck. The surgeon recommended a procedure called an anteriocervical dissection and inner-body fusion. They would take bone from my hip and put it into my spinal column, through my neck. Basically they'd connect my hip bone to my neck bone.

After receiving this news, I was sorely tempted to crawl into a hole somewhere and hide. I was feeling awfully sorry for myself. It would have been easy to take a leave of absence from my parish work and go off somewhere to wallow in self-pity. But I decided I needed to ask myself how I could step up and stay alive. I delayed the surgery for a week to preside at the wedding of two friends the next weekend. And I had the surgery scheduled for a Monday so I could be back in the pulpit the following Sunday. Sure, I had to cope with a great deal of physical pain, but by staying involved as much as was possible in life and work, I avoided something far worse: emotional and spiritual pain. Staying involved was my way of not only coping, but also avoiding the pitfalls of self pity.

A CABBIE STEPS UP

One of my doctors prescribed painkillers to help me deal with the postsurgical agony from a broken neck. While the drugs did indeed cut the pain, I didn't like the way they left me feeling. Foolishly I decided to stop them cold turkey. I ended up going through a difficult few days of withdrawal and on a longer than usual train ride up from Philadelphia to New York I bottomed out. By the time I got to Manhattan I was wracked with nausea. During a cab ride from Penn Station to my apartment I asked the cabdriver to pull over so I could vomit out the door. She handed me an air sickness bag she had in her glove compartment. Not only that, but when we got to my building she got out to help me to the door. She really stepped up. Three years later I hailed a cab to leave a business meeting and who should stop but my guardian angel cabbie. We looked at each other via the rearview mirror and she said she hoped I was feeling better. I told her I'd never forgotten her kindness and that she had helped inspire me to write this book.

Please don't get me wrong. I'm not telling this story to impress you. I'm just offering this as an example of how I was once able to step up. Throughout the rest of this book I'll be offering lots of other stories from my life that will make it clear

I'm no saint. Stepping up isn't about being prideful. It's not about winning some kind of race. There's no competition for who steps up the most, or steps up the furthest. You're not stepping up to get some kind of trophy or plaque. But this isn't something to be overly humble about either. Forced humility has a funny way of turning into false pride. Stepping up is about becoming all you're capable of being in your work, your home, and your soul. It's about discovering what makes you unique and then fulfilling that discovery by doing the hard work of stepping up.

What would it look like if we stepped up?

Let's go back to those examples from earlier in the chapter and see what it would look like if the individuals did the hard work of stepping up.

If you recall, Monica Van Dorn is the charming assistant vice president of an insurance company who has been standing still, letting her boss hold her back from being all she could be. Stepping up for Monica might begin with her realizing she's partially responsible for her situation. Then she could expose her vulnerability and reach out to people outside of work for help in finding someone who could give her professional guidance. Finally, she could step up by actually calling and seeing the career counselor or executive coach. As psychiatrist Carl Jung once said, "One is always in the dark about one's own personality. One needs others to get to know one's self."

I could have stepped up for the not-for-profit on whose board I sit. As I explained earlier, I stepped aside by suggesting someone else chair the organization's task force on diversity. Stepping up in this case might have involved my taking the person I suggested aside and offering to serve as an unofficial sounding board, helping him as much as possible. That way I'd really have been stepping up not just for the organization, but for him too.

Peter Greenberg, the head of research and development who was stepping back to block his perceived rival from succeeding during a leadership summit, could have stepped up instead. That might have meant offering his ideas in a less antagonistic manner. Instead of engaging in back-channel criticisms, he could publicly have said he saw real merits in his rival's proposals, but felt compelled, for the sake of the company, to raise some concerns. And then he could have given his competitor a chance to address the points. Not only would that have been the right thing to do, but it would have improved his own image.

Finally, there's Terry Smith, the programming executive who stepped on his consultant friend by damning her with faint praise when other executives approached him for a referral. In stepping up, he might have stressed that his situation was unique, then added that the consultant was a big help to him and would probably be able to do good work for others in their own situations as well. By stepping up in that manner he could have retained the credit for his success, while helping the consultant, the other executives, and the company as a whole.

STEPPING UP WHILE BEING TAKEN DOWN

Sometimes stepping up is an attitude more than anything else. I think Kevin Blanchard typifies that phenomenon. Kevin served with my son John in Iraq. He and other Marines were in a vehicle that was struck by a roadside bomb. Kevin lost his leg. When I was visiting Kevin after he'd returned stateside at Bethesda Medical Center, he was fielding dozens of telephone calls from friends asking him to look forward to coming out with them to party to celebrate his homecoming. After yet another of these calls he hung up the telephone and looked at me with an expression I'll never forget. He told me, "I love those guys but now I know I have something else to do with my life besides party."

The river ahead

What I'm trying to say to you is this: It's easier to know what you should do than it is to actually do it. Harder still is making stepping up a regular part of your life. Over the years I've found that the best way to internalize this approach to work and life is to fully understand all the options you have, and figure out when and why you choose each. That's why I've structured the rest of the book around the five options you have in every workplace situation: standing still, stepping aside, stepping back, stepping on someone, and stepping up.

In the following five chapters I'll separately discuss each option and explore why we choose it. As in this chapter, I'll provide real-life examples drawn from the lives of those whom

I've counseled, whether as a priest, a negotiator, or a business consultant. I'll also offer examples from my own life and the lives of famous people and historic figures.

Once you finish this book, you'll be convinced, as I am, that stepping up can be a powerful tool of empowerment and ful-fillment. I like to think of myself as being like a river guide. All I can do is draw a map for you. I can point out the rapids and the shallows and indicate where you might have to portage. In these pages I'll point you in a direction. But the paddling is your responsibility. I can't bring you contentment or satisfac-tion. Only one person has that power: you. It won't be easy, but I can tell you from personal experience, it will make all the dif-ference in how you see yourself and the world. Step up and you'll never need to ask if your life mattered. You'll know it has.

There's a wonderful story that, I think, fits our situation. There was a famous daredevil who, having decided to do something really spectacular, went to a major waterfall and set up a wire across the gorge. Word spread quickly, and soon per-haps a thousand people were standing around, waiting for something to happen. Suddenly, the daredevil jumped onto the wire. The crowd started shouting encouragement. And with their cheers echoing, he walked from one side of the falls to the other, then back again. When he finished, the crowd went wild. Inspired by the crowd, the daredevil pulled out a unicycle and started to head across the wire while riding. He started out fine, but then stopped about six feet out. The crowd was hushed but suddenly one man yelled, "Go for it! Don't give up! We know you can do it!" The daredevil slowly pedaled back to where the crowd had gathered. He looked around until he found the man who had shouted the encouraging words. "Do you really think I can do this?" he asked. The man in the crowd yelled back, "Yes. I really believe in you. I believe you can do it! Go for it!" The daredevil smiled. Looking at the encouraging man in the crowd, he said, "If you really believe I can do it, get on my shoulders and come with me."

So get off the sidelines, get into the game, and come for a ride. It's a bit dangerous, but nothing like crossing a major waterfall on a wire while on the back of a unicyclist. And believe me, the views—and the experience—are worth it.

2

Standing Still

The worst sin towards our fellow creatures is not to hate them, but to be indifferent to them; that's the essence of inhumanity.

—George Bernard Shaw

Do something. I know it can be hard. And it may seem risky. But to step up and experience meaning in your work and life, you'll first need to stop standing still.

To stand still is to do nothing. Standing still means inaction or indifference. We all stand still most of the time. Whether it's at work or at home, whenever we're facing a situation that requires us to make a choice, most times we stand still and do nothing; it's the default option. Let's say you're in line at the ATM and you see someone cut in ahead. Most of us just let it happen. We may seethe inside or even mutter under our breath, but usually we stand still and do nothing. Or perhaps you're in a meeting at work and one of your coworkers promises delivery of a report by a deadline you know is simply impossible. Rather than diplomatically interjecting a caution, or pulling the individual aside for a quick chat after the meeting, you just let it happen. Standing still doesn't necessarily mean physical inactivity. It could just as easily manifest itself as emotional indifference, or spiritual apathy: we see someone desperately trying to place a bag in the overhead rack of an airplane and we stay seated, pretending we don't see the struggle; or we hear about a coworker who has suffered a trauma and we just tune it out.

Don't feel guilty if you recognize yourself in these examples. Standing still is human nature. Trying to overcome that natural indifference forms the basis of most of our religious traditions. The poet W. H. Auden once wrote, "We are not commanded (or forbidden) to love our mates, our children, our friends, our country because such affections come naturally to us and are good in themselves, although we may corrupt them. We are commanded to love our neighbor because our 'natural' attitude toward the 'other' is one of either indifference or hostility."

THE POOL OF BETHESDA (JOHN 5:1–8)

Jesus came to Jerusalem for a festival and went to visit the pool of Bethesda, where great numbers of disabled people gathered because the waters were said to be miraculous. The belief was that an angel appeared at times to stir the pool, and the first person to enter after the stirring was healed. As he walked to the pool, Jesus spoke with one invalid, begging alongside the pool, who said he had been lying there for thirty-eight years. Jesus asked, "Do you want to get well?" The man said he did, but that every time an angel stirred the pool, he was beaten into the water. Jesus told the man, "Get up! Pick up your mat and walk." The man was cured.

Perhaps the invalid really was beaten into the pool for

thirty-eight years. But maybe, just maybe, he was happy to stand still, or actually, lie still. The pool at Bethesda was a popular spot and the invalid probably did quite well begging there. It was easier for him to stay where he was than to drag himself across the ground. Besides, if he got up, he risked losing his livelihood. All he'd known for thirty-eight years was begging at the pool. Jesus confronted him with his standing still and urged him to take responsibility for himself. The invalid did and was able to step up.

Standing still is so much a part of us that most times we do it without even thinking. In the early summer of 2005 while I was working on this book, I was walking down the street in Manhattan on my way home after a meeting at a client's office. It had been a long and intense meeting, and I was running late for dinner with a friend. Out of the corner of my eye I saw a large, irregularly shaped object on the ground in front of a telephone booth. I did a double take and saw it was a person, lying there, unmoving. I slowed for a second or two to check that the fellow was breathing, and when I saw he was, I picked up the pace and went on my way. Later that night after a couple of glasses of wine, I flashed back to that encounter. Twenty years ago I would never have walked by that person. It wouldn't have mattered how badly he smelled, or how much of a hurry I was in; I would have stopped to see if I could be of help. I don't know whether it's because I'm older, I'm more concerned with contagious diseases, I'm suffering from compassion burnout, or if years of city living has built a protective shell around my soul. Ever since, I've been exploring that with my coaches and confessors. But whatever the reason, I definitely "stood still" reflexively and kept on walking when I should have stepped up by stopping to see if I could have helped that man lying on the sidewalk.

Sometimes we rationalize standing still by thinking someone else will step up so we don't need to. One of the most disturbing crime stories of the 1960s was the case of Kitty Genovese. At about 3:15 a.m. on March 13, 1964, Kitty returned home from her job as the manager of a bar. The outgoing, petite twenty-eight-year-old parked her car twenty feet from the door to her apartment in the Kew Gardens section of Queens, New York. She was suddenly attacked by a man with a knife who had been prowling the area. As she screamed, some lights came on in the windows of the apartment buildings surrounding the scene. One man yelled at the attacker and he ran off. Bleeding badly, Kitty dragged herself to the doorway of her apartment. She cried out that she was dying, but no one came to her aid. The attacker returned, sexually assaulted the now semiconscious Kitty, stabbed her again, and killed her. It took more than thirty minutes for a bystander to telephone the police, and he did so only after first calling a friend and asking for advice. During the investigation the New York Police Department determined that no fewer than thirty-eight people heard or observed the killing without calling the police. For years psychologists have theorized why thirty-eight people just stood still. The most compelling theory involves the bystander effect, which postulates that as the number of bystanders increases, the sense of personal responsibility decreases, and as a result, so does the likelihood of anyone stepping up.

———

America makes prodigious mistakes, America

has colossal faults, but one thing cannot be

denied: America is always on the move. She

may be going to Hell, of course, but at least

she isn't standing still.

—e. e. cummings

———

Other times we tell ourselves standing still is the best thing we could do. Herbert Hoover was orphaned at age eleven. He put himself through college, married, and moved to China, where he became a successful engineer. During World War One, Hoover became an international figure leading relief efforts for the millions starving in war-torn Europe. His renown led to appointments to the cabinets of presidents Warren Harding and Calvin Coolidge and then to his own election as president in 1928. When the stock market crashed in 1929, leading to the Great Depression, Hoover's response was to rely on volunteerism and nongovernmental efforts to turn the economy around. Hoover believed government intervention would destroy Americans' individuality and self-reliance. He thought it would be better for government to do nothing. Under his leadership, facing the greatest economic crisis in the

nation's history, his administration stood still rather than stepping up. It's one of the great ironies of history that a man who
became president largely due to his charitable efforts is remembered today as callous and uncaring.

Whether we stand still without thinking, as I did when
walking past that man on the street, or we somehow rationalize the behavior, as did the bystanders to the Kitty Genovese
murder and Herbert Hoover about his failure to respond ag-
gressively to the Great Depression, it's almost always the worst
thing we could do. Inaction and indifference can be the worst
of sins. It's better to do something, anything, than nothing. It's
better to get angry at someone or something than to not care
at all.

**The only thing necessary for the triumph of
evil is for good men to do nothing.**

—Edmund Burke

I may not yet know exactly why I stood still when I saw that
homeless man lying on the sidewalk, but I've learned there are
four reasons why, in general, we all stand still: it's the easiest
path to follow; it's the safest choice; it's been part of our upbringing; or perhaps we feel we've already done our share of
stepping up.

THE EASIEST CHOICE

Standing still is the easiest response in any situation. Action of any kind, whether it's proactive or reactive, supportive or contrary, requires the exertion of physical or emotional energy. Standing still, on the other hand, requires no exertion. It was Sir Isaac Newton who first theorized the law of physics that an object at rest will stay at rest unless acted on by an unbalanced force. I believe that goes for mental as well as physical rest. Physically and spiritually it's easiest for us just to stand still.

It's especially easy to stand still when you have a degree of material comfort and success. Perhaps it's because, having never experienced real want, or maybe having gone a long time without feeling it, we lose our compassion for those in need. We either don't know or have forgotten what it's like. I think that's why the percentage of income individuals donate to charity is inversely proportionate to wealth: the less someone has, the greater portion of their money they give to others. I came face-to-face with the tendency of those with wealth to stand still back when I was pastor of an affluent parish on the "Main Line" of Philadelphia. My wife and I had moved into the rectory along with our two sons and our dog. While it was a beautiful old house, the fence around the yard was dilapidated, making it dangerous for the boys and the dog to play back there. I went to the head of the parish committee responsible for upkeep of the facilities and asked them to approve installation of a new fence. It would have cost around $1,000.

THE WORST SIN

I've always thought Charles Baudelaire's poem "To the Reader" a powerful exploration of the worst of evils. Here are the lines that have always stayed with me:

And yet, among the beasts and creatures all—
Panther, snake, scorpion, jackal, ape, hound, hawk—
Monsters that crawl, and shriek, and grunt, and squawk,
In our vice-filled menagerie's caterwaul,
One worse is there, fit to heap scorn upon—
More ugly, rank! Though noiseless, calm and still,
Yet would he turn the earth to scraps and swill,
Swallow it whole in one great, gaping yawn:
Ennui! That monster frail!—With eye wherein
A chance tear gleams, he dreams of gibbets, while
Smoking his hookah, with a dainty smile . . .
—You know him, reader,—hypocrite,—my twin!

The chairman of the committee, a man I'll call Paul Lyman, was, like quite a few in the parish, heir to a family fortune. Paul had held few jobs other than serving as a board member of the church and of a number of other organizations his family had supported over the years. When I approached Paul about the fence, he acted as if I were asking him to fund a manned mission to Mars. "Do you really need a fence?" he asked at first. After I pointed out that I had two young sons and a dog in a house right off a major thoroughfare, he grudgingly conceded it might be necessary. But then he asked, "Couldn't we just repair it?" He was looking for every possible way to stand still just to make things easier.

The safest choice

This law of physics is amplified by the fact that standing still is, at least superficially, the safest choice. It's human nature to believe things could always get worse. Sure, standing still in your current situation may not be perfect, but nothing is, right? So, any action could lead to things getting worse. Action means change. And change means risk. That means it's safer to do nothing. Most of us seem to believe in the old Irish proverb "Better the devil you know than the devil you don't know."

STEPPING UP TO PAY BACK CONFIDENCE

There's a wonderful example of both standing still and stepping up in the 1955 film *Mister Roberts*. Throughout the movie, Mister Roberts (played by Henry Fonda), the executive officer of a cargo ship in World War Two, is stepping up to protect the crew from the ship's despotic captain, Morton (played by James Cagney). Roberts, who is desperately trying to transfer to a combat vessel, encourages a junior officer, Ensign Pulver (played by Jack Lemmon), to also step up for the crew. Pulver, however, scared by the captain's bluster and threats, always stands still. Roberts finally manages a transfer and the crew loses its defender. Pulver continues to just stand still. Then, two letters arrive. One, an official notice, announces that Rob-

erts has died in action. The other is Roberts's final letter. In it
he writes that "the unseen enemy of this war is the boredom
that eventually becomes a faith and, therefore, a terrible sort
of suicide. And I know now that the ones who refuse to surrender to it are the strongest of all." After a moment's reflection,
Pulver, inspired by Roberts's words and example, finally steps
up for the crew and demands they get time off.

Thomas Kaplow, thirty-seven, has had a difficult few years.
Thomas, a storklike man with a dark brown ponytail, is a brilliant mathematician who gave up an academic career to work
as an actuary with an international insurance company. For a
few years things were going well for him, his wife, and their
young daughter. As a pediatrician, Thomas's wife brought in
just as much money as he did. But after a few years things began getting rocky. Both Thomas and his wife placed their ca-
reers ahead of their marriage. Then, just as they seemed to
have weathered their marital difficulties, Thomas was diagnosed with multiple sclerosis.

While his condition didn't preclude his working, Thomas
quit his job. His wife's patience, already worn thin, soon
snapped. She and Thomas separated. As the months passed,
Thomas became comfortable in his misery. It is now safer for
him to stay unemployed and alone than to step up and assume
some risk by confronting his physical and psychological ob-
stacles. Currently receiving public assistance and refusing
counseling, Thomas is insisting on standing still.

Throughout history it has been the inaction of those who could have acted, the indifference of those who should have known better, the silence of the voice of justice when it mattered most, that has made it possible for evil to triumph.

—Haile Selassie

The choice we're taught

Some of us were raised to do nothing. When some children start acting independently, they're told in no uncertain terms to stop: "Don't touch anything. Don't talk to strangers. Just sit quietly." As soon as they're capable of stepping up, they're told to conform, to not rock the boat, to follow the pack, to stand still. These early lessons, unless overcome, can serve as a foundation for a lifelong pattern of standing still.

Naomi Green, forty-three, an intense, bespectacled woman with closely cropped brown hair, has been married to her husband, Seth, for twenty years. For the past ten years they've also worked together as owners of a film distribution company specializing in bringing independent American films to European markets. Their business, started as a lark right after they'd both graduated film school, has become extremely successful. So, she used to think, was their marriage. Brought together not just by the mutual love of film, but their religiously observant backgrounds, the couple and their three children were fixtures in their suburban community. Outwardly their lives seemed right on course. That's why I was so surprised when I ran into Naomi, whom I knew from previous consulting work, at a corporate seminar I was attending. She looked as if she'd just lost a loved one.

Naomi pulled me aside and asked if she could speak with me privately. "You're a minister," she began, "tell me what to do." She then told me she had fallen madly in love with one of her company's other executives. He felt the same. I asked if they had acted on their attraction. "How could I do that?" she asked. "I'm married. We can't split up. I have kids and we're pillars of the community." Raised with strong values of faith and fidelity, Naomi couldn't act on her feelings. Instead, she stood still and remained true to her idea of self.

The choice we made once before

Finally, some of us use our prior instances of stepping up as a rationalization for now standing still. Having at least once exerted energy, taken a risk, and overcome childhood conditioning to do the right thing, we feel we've now earned our spurs and can stand still without guilt. Rather than seeing stepping up as a way of living in the world, we view it as a right of passage or a "get out of responsibility free" card.

Sharon Greenstein is one of my favorite clients. The fifty-six-year-old vivacious executive is known throughout the not-for-profit industry in the mid-Atlantic city where she works and lives. Sharon began her working life as a social worker but moved into management after going back to college to earn her doctorate in public policy. I first met her when I was called in to help her manage the merger of two nonprofit agencies with nearly identical missions, but with quite different cultures. Sharon was brought in from the outside to take over one of the divisions of the newly formed organization. Her years "in the trenches" had instilled in her a vision of what an agency should be like. When she and I first met, she explained to me that social workers needed to feel that their agency "had their backs covered." Overworked and underpaid, social workers were subject to early burnout and disillusionment. She told me she wanted the organization's primary mission to be maintaining the morale of its social workers in the field, knowing that would translate into better results for the agency's clients. It was a gamble and an uphill fight, but Sharon stepped up and led a recalcitrant board and cynical leadership team into building a truly extraordinary division.

Sharon's success in her division turned her into a rising star in the agency. She's now seen by the board as a possible successor to the agency's current director, who's due to retire in three years. I was recently called in to facilitate a leadership summit for the agency. It soon became clear to me that the agency's other two divisions—analysis and development—were in desperate need of the same kind of morale improvement Sharon had led in her own division. During a break in the summit Sharon and I spoke about it. She immediately agreed with my assessment and told me that she had, in fact, made similar comments to a couple of members of the board. But since the other two divisions were staffed by researchers and fund-raisers rather than social workers, the board members didn't accept the similarity. When I asked how she'd responded to their denial, she shrugged. "I've already stuck my head out here," she said. "In all honesty I've accomplished more and climbed higher than I thought I ever would. It's time for some-one else to step up."

In some ways, I find situations like Sharon's the saddest, al-beit the most understandable. Sure, she deserves all sorts of credit for having stepped up. And everyone needs a bit of a break—even Jesus said it was fine for Mary to anoint his feet with precious oil rather than sell the oil and spend the money on the poor. But having seen all the good that can come of it, and having experienced the sense of meaning it can bring to her life, Sharon has chosen to rest on her laurels. She's just one step away from a true renaissance—making stepping up a per-manent part of her life—but isn't ready yet to go that final mile. The urge to stand still is so powerful that even those who've stepped up in the past, and experienced all its extraor-dinary results, still succumb. That goes for our personal lives as well as our work lives.

THE ULTIMATE CASE OF STANDING STILL

There's no more horrifying example of standing still than the world's response to the Holocaust. World leaders who had stepped up against great odds to battle fascism stood still while the genocide of Europe's Jews took place. Historians continue to debate the reasons for the inaction, and what could actually have been done. But there's no debate about the impact of the world's standing still. As the writer Elie Wiesel, himself a Holocaust survivor, has written, "The opposite of love is not hate, it's indifference. The opposite of art is not ugliness, it's indifference. The opposite of faith is not heresy, it's indifference. And the opposite of life is not death, it's indifference." And standing still doesn't just allow others to suffer, it leads to our own suffering. As Wiesel has also written, "Because of indifference, one dies before one actually dies." I wish I could say the world had learned this lesson.

"I just can't do it!"

Matthew James, a forty-seven-year-old high school teacher and football coach, was always the "good son." His older brother, Peter, a fifty-one-year-old dentist, had a distant, sometimes antagonistic relationship with their widowed mother, Fiona. Peter and his wife lived less than an hour away from Fiona. Matthew, who was close to his mother, had moved with his wife to a small college town about two hundred miles away. Despite the distance, a four-hour drive, Matthew and his wife were always there for his mother through the years.

Fiona, an active seventy-three-year-old, called Matthew late one night to break the news that she had breast cancer. Matthew and his wife immediately drove down to be with Fiona.

During the two weeks between Fiona's initial diagnosis and surgery, Matthew just about commuted between his job and his childhood home four hours away. Peter, while not as emotionally supportive of Fiona as Matthew, bore his share of the chores and tasks. It was agreed that after the surgery Fiona would stay with Peter and his wife until she was well enough to go home and take care of herself. But when the time came for Fiona to leave the hospital, all the pent-up emotions burst forth and things began to go awry.

Fiona called Matthew early one morning at work to tell him she had no way of getting from the hospital to Peter's house. She said Peter had told her that neither he nor his wife could make the drive to and from the hospital, and that she should instead call Matthew and ask him to pick her up and drop her off. Matthew's jaw dropped. He couldn't believe his brother expected him to drive eight hours round-trip to transport his mother on a forty-minute trip. All the frustration and anger that had built up within Matthew over the past month exploded. He railed about his brother on the phone to his mother, who responded with tears and cries that she didn't know what to do. Matthew said he didn't know either, but added, "I just can't do it." He explained he had to get back to work and hung up the telephone. He purposely didn't call his mother back that evening.

The next morning Matthew got a call from Fiona. After getting off the telephone with Matthew, she had been in tears. A nurse contacted a hospital social worker, who soon arrived in the room. The social worker helped Fiona work through the situation. Rather than going to Peter's house, Fiona arranged for a health care aide to come stay with her in her own home. She also called a local taxi company and arranged for a car to pick her up at the hospital and drop her off at home. Matthew, while glad his mother had taken charge of her own life, still feels guilty he stood still rather than step up.

Apathy is one of the characteristic responses of any living organism when it is subjected to stimuli too intense or too complicated to cope with. The cure for apathy is comprehension.

—John Dos Passos

"But we're such a good team"

There's still a great deal of standing still in the workplace. A few years ago I worked with a wonderful group of people in the fulfillment department of a large consumer products company in the Midwest. The president of the corporation had heard me give a presentation at a conference sponsored by the

Wharton School and asked me to work with him in developing a healthier culture at his company.

The fulfillment department was held out to me as the "healthiest" part of the company. The manager of the department was historically a candidate for higher corporate office, and the current director was no exception. He was a competent if cold fellow named Bob Radcliffe. An Ivy League MBA with an eye for detail, he was focused on the bottom line while remaining fair to his staff. It was the staff that made the department. Debbie Romano, twenty-five, Phyllis Dietrich, twenty-three, Tanya Green, twenty-two, and Lisa Buckner, also twenty-two, seemed more like sisters than coworkers. All were recent graduates from the undergraduate business-school programs at some of the nation's better universities. While they came from different parts of the country and different backgrounds, they seemed to mesh perfectly. Their good humor and camaraderie transformed that section of the building, despite its being just another collection of enclosed workstations, into a happy place. There was laughter, conversation, and enthusiasm, even though the work they were actually doing could be quite tedious. They routinely ate lunch together and often went out for drinks after work. The four women would frequently work late, and Bob always made sure to pick up the tab for pizza and sodas.

The problem was there was no place for them to go in the company. Even though management of the department had always been a stepping-stone to higher positions, no one within the department had ever been promoted to head it up. Not only that, but few workers in the department had ever been able even to shift laterally. Rather than an example of a healthy culture, the department was actually an example of one of the things that was wrong with the organization: there weren't opportunities for smart, young people to grow. Ironically, the fulfillment department offered no opportunities for its members to get fulfillment. When I approached management about the issue, I was told there simply wasn't any advancement track for these people in-house. To grow professionally they'd either have to leave the company or make retrograde moves to another department. I tried gently discussing this with the four women and ran into a charming brick wall. They so enjoyed each other's company that they were each standing still. Debbie, the most senior of the four, was beginning to realize something was wrong. But when I subtly asked her about looking for other opportunities, she winced and said, "But we're such a good team."

"I'm too embarrassed"

I was once part of a good team too. There were several of us, but I will only refer to a few: me, Scott, Tracy, Ray, Bob, Dave, Pat, and David. Growing up in Gainesville, Florida, we were inseparable. We went through all the typical coming-of-age milestones together: school, sports, rock and roll, and relationships—not necessarily in that order. And we were all involved in some sort of social service outreach with inner-city kids. After graduation we'd get in touch now and then, but as the years passed those contacts became fewer and further apart. By the time we'd entered our thirties our contact had drifted away. Every once in a while I'd hear about something happening in their lives—a marriage, a birth, the death of a parent, a divorce—and think about calling, but I never did.

————————

Every time we turn our heads the other way when we see the law flouted—when we tolerate what we know to be wrong—when we close our eyes and ears to the corrupt because we are too busy, or too frightened—when we fail to speak up and speak out—we strike a blow against freedom and decency and justice.

—Robert F. Kennedy

————————

Then a few years ago my mother, who still lives in Gainesville, called to tell me David had suffered a heart attack. Could there be a more perfect reason for someone, especially a priest, to get back in touch? This was one of the closest friends I'd had in my life, and even though we hadn't been in touch, he still occupied a huge place in my heart. Over the years I've gone out of my way to be there for people going through traumatic times, even if we didn't know each other and only knew of each other. Yet when I heard about David's heart attack, I didn't pick up the telephone. My mother sounded genuinely puzzled when she asked me why I hadn't called, why I had stood still when one of my oldest and dearest friends was in need. All I could say was "I'm too embarrassed."

TOO CLOSE TO REACH OUT

In the summer of 2005, in one terrible week more than twenty U.S. Marines were killed in Iraq. The news was filled with the story, each time noting the unit involved . . . in which my son John served. John came through that week unscathed, but it was a difficult time for all of the families at home waiting to hear the details.

During that week, as the news reports kept coming in, only a handful of people stepped up to call and check in with me. One was a new colleague who was working with me on a major project. Another was an executive at a client company. The others were a group of young women whose offices are outside the office I occasionally use when working on-site at one of my clients. My mother didn't call. My brother didn't call. Close friends didn't call.

Now, I'm as guilty of that kind of standing still as anyone— just read this chapter. So I'm not looking to criticize those who didn't call. I just thought it surprising that those who were closest to me didn't call, while a handful of people who weren't as close did reach out. I think sometimes we use our closeness to someone as a rationalization for standing still. They know we're thinking of them, we tell ourselves. Besides, it's easier and less risky not to make a potentially difficult call. Meanwhile, some people who don't take closeness for granted, also don't take stepping up for granted. I guess the message is, you're never too close to reach out.

What would it look like if we stepped up?

Paul Lyman could have "overcome" his wealth and shown that he put the safety of his pastor's family over an expense smaller than his monthly greens fees. He could have stepped up, even though it wasn't the easiest thing to do, and agreed to a new fence right away, rather than first making me feel like a supplicant. He would have made a difference in not just my family's life, but perhaps in his own as well. Who knows? Maybe he would have seen that small acts of human kindness can be just as, if not more, rewarding than having your family's name inscribed on an impersonal marble cornerstone.

Thomas Kaplow doesn't need to stand still even though he has MS. Sure, it would be a risk to go back into the workplace with his disability. It might be humbling, maybe even humiliating, at first. But if he starts to engage in the world again and takes responsibility for himself, he'll see his life can still have meaning, and he can bring meaning to others' lives as well, if not directly then perhaps through his example.

Naomi Green can try to overcome her conservative upbringing. Whatever direction her heart and soul direct her, she needs to step up, and get some therapy or counseling. Whether after counseling she decides to make a go of it with her husband or to start over with someone else, she needs to step up for all their sakes. Letting community mores and attitudes keep her standing still is making her miserable. If she steps up, she can, in the long term, bring meaning to her life and to the lives of those around her.

Sure, Sharon Greenstein deserves kudos for having stepped up in the past at her nonprofit. But if she lets that keep her standing still, she's missing an incredible opportunity to get to the next level of personal development, as well as the next rung on the corporate ladder. Stepping up and trying to make things better for the company and its employees is always the right thing to do. What would be the point of climbing higher if she doesn't intend to use the added power to do good? Here's a chance for her to bring meaning to an entire company. Think of what that could do for her soul.

Neither the good son, Matthew James, the four young women in the fulfillment department, nor me and my old buddy needed to stand still. We too could have stepped up and brought greater meaning not just to our own lives, but to the lives of others.

Matthew could have set aside his anger with his brother and his frustration with his mother's not taking charge of her situation. That doesn't mean he should have driven eight hours to transport her on a forty-minute ride. But he could have talked her through the process and helped her go through all her options and decide what to do.

The four young women at the consumer products company could have stepped up as well. Sure, it's fun for them to be together and to have such wonderful camaraderie, but by standing still they're not growing either as individuals or professionals. There's no opportunity for them to advance in that department. They could each look for other jobs in other departments or outside the company while still trying to maintain contact.

As for me, I could have stepped up and been there for my friend David when he had his heart attack. All it would have taken was a telephone call. I think I might have been of some help to him in a difficult time. But I was too wrapped up in my own guilt. My story doesn't end there, however. A few years ago my father died, and while letting people know of his passing, I called three of my old friends, including David. We all spoke about getting together, but once again I stood still. But David stepped up. He followed up with all of us, made the telephone calls and wrote the e-mails to make it all happen. In the two years since then we've all gotten together twice: once for a weekend in Philadelphia, and subsequently for a fishing trip in Florida. David didn't stand still. He stepped up and improved all our lives.

STEPPING UP BY STANDING STILL

At times you may need to consciously stand still to step up. That was true for Stu Titlebaum, fifty-three. Stu is one of the most giving, compassionate, caring individuals I've ever met. He's an extraordinarily successful entrepreneur who has done well for himself financially. Stu is always involved in philanthropic programs in New York City, where he lives and works, and in other less formal efforts to help those less fortunate than himself. He's also generous to his family and friends. That personal generosity led to a conflict he told me he was having.

Stu comes from a solidly middle-class family. His younger brother, Aaron, forty-nine, is also a successful entrepreneur, in Florida. Their parents also live in Florida, in a retirement community. One day when I was meeting with Stu about an executive retreat we were planning, he told me how disappointed he was with his brother. Stu and Aaron's father had been ill in recent years, and Stu, being Stu, had arranged for the top medical specialists to treat his dad. He'd hired a nurse to stay with his father when he came home after surgery. Stu paid for the parents' condo to be redecorated, in an effort to raise their spirits. Now he was planning to send them both on a cruise holiday. When he called his parents to finalize the vacation plans, he casually asked when was the last time they'd seen Aaron. They mentioned that while he'd called, he hadn't stopped by for more than a month. Stu told me he was ticked off that his brother hadn't been stepping up for his parents.

After hearing the whole story, I asked Stu to look at things from a slightly different perspective. I asked Stu if maybe his efforts on behalf of his parents hadn't left any room for Aaron to step up. Stu said he had never looked at it that way and told me he'd give it some thought.

When I met with Stu two weeks later, he said he had good news. During a telephone conversation a few days before he'd learned his parents were having a problem with their car. He almost reflexively jumped into the breach again, but instead, he gave it a moment's thought. Stu suggested that his parents give Aaron a call and ask for his advice and help instead. A few days later he learned that Aaron had not only helped answer their questions, but had arranged for their car to be repaired and had picked up the cost. By consciously standing still, Stu stepped up by finally giving his brother a chance to step up too.

3

Stepping Aside

Without a vision, the people perish.

—Proverbs 29:18a

If there's one thing this book is meant to convey it is this: take responsibility. Stop blaming others for where you find yourself in both your personal and professional lives. Step up and become aware of your power to impact your world. Don't purposely schedule a business meeting so your sister has to take Mom to the doctor's office on her own. Don't call in sick so your colleague has to face the irate executive vice president on his own. When you step aside and force, maneuver, or allow someone else to tackle an obstacle, you're missing an opportunity to step up and make a difference.

If standing still is inaction or indifference, stepping aside is avoidance or abdication. When you stand still, you're not sure what needs to be done, nor if you could do it. You simply don't want to get involved, so instead you do nothing. Stepping aside is an error of omission. You're facing a situation in which you know something must be done, and you realize you have the opportunity to do it, but instead you let someone else step up. You see what needs to be done and are aware you could do it, but you lack the vision that you have a responsibility to do it.

THE SIN OF OMISSION

There's a wonderful poem by Margaret Sangster, titled "The Sin of Omission," that I think explains stepping aside far better than I ever could. Here is one particularly powerful stanza.

It isn't the thing you do, dear;
It's the thing you leave undone,
That gives you a bit of heartache
At setting of the sun.
The tender word forgotten,
The letter you did not write,
The flowers you did not send, dear,
Are your haunting ghosts to-night.

You step aside at work when you fail to address a problem or potential problem as soon as it becomes apparent and, instead, leave it for someone else to handle. Let's say you sell advertising space for a magazine. You've worked long and hard to land a quarter-page ad from a particularly recalcitrant customer. When the materials finally arrive, you notice the ad is the wrong size and shape. But rather than call the customer to solve the problem, you leave it to the production manager to make the difficult telephone call.

You step aside in your personal life when you see potential conflict or difficulties and either delay or maneuver so you're out of the line of fire. Maybe you've learned your teenage son wants to travel to Florida with three of his high school buddies for spring break . . . and he'd like to take one of the family vehicles. Rather than be the "bad guy" and raise all the issues that concern you, you remain noncommittal, knowing that when your spouse arrives home later, she'll reflexively respond the way you hope.

THE BUCK STOPS WITH YOU

At times, all of us, rather than doing what we think or feel or know needs to be done, step aside and let someone else shoulder the responsibility. Part of this is our innate imperfection. We're all human, so sometimes we don't measure up to our best selves. That said, I think society has become far less responsible in recent years.

There are plenty of recommendations on how to get out of trouble cheaply and fast. Most of them come down to this: Deny your responsibility.

—Lyndon Baines Johnson

President Harry Truman had a sign on his desk that read THE BUCK STOPS HERE. But few of our subsequent world leaders seem to have lived up to Truman's motto. For example, many believe the 1994 slaughter of over eight hundred thousand Rwandans was preventable. In fact, an international commission initiated by the Organization of African Unity condemned the Clinton administration, France, the U.N. Security Council and Secretariat, Belgium, and the Roman Catholic Church for failing to prevent or stop the genocide.

Another world leader provides a more direct and personal example of stepping aside: Richard Nixon. When news of the Watergate break-in first began to appear in the *Washington Post* and other newspapers, President Nixon was faced with a choice. He could have stepped up and taken responsibility for those who'd conducted a "third-rate burglary." Undoubtedly he would have suffered politically. For whatever reason, Nixon chose to step aside instead, letting a series of aides and operatives take the fall in an effort to cover up the truth and derail the investigation. When one aide, White House counsel John Dean, refused to continue participating in the cover-up, the truth began to emerge. Historians debate what would have happened had Nixon stepped up and assumed responsibility early on. But there's no debate that his stepping aside resulted in his being the only U.S. president forced to resign.

In many ways, Nixon's choice is emblematic of a societal trend. It's been important for our development as individuals and as a society to try to understand the underlying reasons for problems. That way we can try to break long-term negative patterns in our own behavior and our communities. But we've grown comfortable with blaming others and letting ourselves off the hook. The six words I've heard the least in all my years of pastoral and executive counseling are "I'm sorry—it was my fault." I believe we were created with free will, and because of this we're responsible not just for ourselves, but for the world around us.

The British critic Cyril Connolly once wrote, "We create the world in which we live; if that world becomes unfit for human life, it is because we tire of our responsibility." Obviously I don't mean you're personally responsible for hunger in Haiti or genocide in Darfur. All humanity is collectively responsible for such horrors. Individually you're responsible for doing the best you can, for being aware, for making the loving choice, for stepping up.

One of the annoying things about believing in free will and individual responsibility is the difficulty of finding somebody to blame your problems on. And when you do find somebody, it's remarkable how often his picture turns up on your driver's license.

—P. J. O'Rourke

There are, unfortunately, millions of horrible real-life examples of stepping aside. But sometimes fictional stories serve to drive home the point by painting archetypes for us. One such portrayal comes from the television series *The Sopranos*. Christopher Moltisanti, the impulsive nephew and subordinate of mob leader Tony Soprano, faced a difficult choice. He discovered that his fiancée, Adriana La Cerva, had been pressured by the FBI to be an informer on the Soprano crime family. Over the many years of their relationship Adriana had shown Christopher that she loved him unconditionally. She encouraged him to pursue his ill-conceived goal of becoming a scriptwriter. Adriana was there for Christopher when he sank into heroin addiction and struggled through rehab. Looking for the same kind of support from Christopher, Adriana confessed her FBI problem and asked him to run away with her. While at first he seemed prepared to step up for Adriana, Christopher began to think what life would be like for them outside of organized crime. Faced with choosing between his fiancée and his lifestyle, Christopher tells Tony of Adriana's link to the FBI and steps aside, allowing her to be killed.

Stepping aside isn't reserved for lawbreakers. One of the best examples comes from classical literature and one of Western civilization's greatest heroes.

While the Greeks sailing to wage war on the Trojans are formally led by Agamemnon, king of Mycenae, their leader on the field of battle is Achilles, king of the Myrmidons, who was the greatest warrior of the age. Homer's *Iliad* begins with the Trojan War already under way. Agamemnon and Achilles are quarreling. Agamemnon, in an effort to assert his primacy, has taken a captive slave girl from Achilles. Achilles sees this as an affront to his honor and angrily decides to withdraw himself and his army from combat. Achilles steps aside, forcing Agamemnon and the other Greeks to face the Trojans alone.

Only when his beloved Patroclus is killed and the Trojans are about to burn the Greek ships and win the war does Achilles step up, join the battle, and beat back the attack.

STEPPING UP BY STAYING TOGETHER

Linda and Millard Fuller seemed to have it all. Millard was a successful businessman, and Linda, after having raised their two children, had just finished the college degree she'd gone back to school to earn. They were in the middle of having an architect design their dream home. But all wasn't as it seemed. Millard admittedly put his business before everything else. The couple had drifted apart and were on the verge of a divorce. They decided to visit a pastor they both knew who lived in New York City. While sitting on the steps of St. Patrick's Cathedral, the couple decided they wanted to make things right and start over rather than split up.

Soon thereafter the couple sold everything they owned, gave the money away, and began working at an African American college. Then they joined a Christian community called Koinonia Farm, where people were trying to apply Christ's teachings in a practical way. After pilot projects in Africa and the southeast United States, the Fullers formed their own organization in 1976 to help develop low-income housing. They named it Habitat for Humanity.

The Clinton administration, Richard Nixon, Christopher Moltisanti, and Achilles all stepped aside, but for different reasons. Nixon, I believe, did so out of self-righteousness. He believed, as he later explained, that if the president of the United States does something, by definition it can't be illegal. One reason the Clinton administration stepped aside was out of fear for the political ramifications for intervening in another African conflict on the heels of its disastrous actions in Somalia. Christopher Moltisanti also stepped aside out of fear, not just of Tony Soprano's wrath, but of losing the comfortable life of crime he'd embraced. Achilles stepped aside out of anger at Agamemnon for disrespecting him. Only an even greater feeling of anger, over the death of Patroclus, later leads him to step up. Those three motivations, self-righteousness, fear, and anger, led the rest of those described in this chapter to step aside as well.

Acting self-righteous

At times we step aside out of self-righteousness. Often this happens when you feel superior to another person in the situation. It could be a child or perhaps a subordinate. It might even be a peer or equal whom you perceive to be less emotionally, morally, or spiritually enlightened than yourself. Rather than stepping up ourselves, we step aside and rationalize our abdication by telling ourselves we're doing the other party a favor by maneuvering him into stepping up. Often we frame it as a lesson that will build his character or a necessary step in his professional growth. That's exactly how Diane Ferguson saw her stepping aside.

Diane and her husband, Philip, both twenty-seven, are on the verge of splitting up. Philip recently declared that he'd "outgrown" Diane and needed to "move on." The two had met in college and got married right after graduation. Diane had wanted to go on to divinity school, while Philip wanted to go to law school. Diane encouraged Philip to go right on to law school and volunteered to get a job to support them, putting her own plans on hold. But within months of Philip's graduating law school and landing a job at a prestigious firm, he made his pronouncement. Diane's bitterness is based at least in part on her having stepped aside and allowed Philip to step up and continue his academic work. Only after a great deal of counseling did Diane realize she is partly complicit since she stepped aside to reinforce her feelings of moral superiority and to try to encourage Philip to be more selfless. Diane may garner the sympathy of her friends and congregation by being seen as the victim of Philip's selfishness, but she will remain stuck in the pity parlor if she refuses to become conscious of her responsibility in the demise of the relationship. Philip, of course, has his own issues.

THE FAILING PARISH

Even those of us who are called to step up sometimes step aside. Charles E. Bennison, the Episcopal bishop of Pennsylvania, tells a poignant story about a parish that was failing. The rector of the parish differed dramatically in attitude and approach from the majority of the congregants, and over time the congregation shrank dramatically.

When it became clear there was a real conflict, without many solutions, the rector was encouraged to resign. The diocese, unwilling to give up on the parish, tried to revive the congregation. Outside diocesan funds were used to revive the church building itself and create new programs. A new vicar was put in place. It was slow going, but things seemed to be on the verge of turning around.

Then, the new vicar stepped aside rather than up. In an open meeting of parishioners the vicar went over all the efforts that had been made and talked about how far the congregation had come. But then he said he thought it wouldn't be enough, and that the community simply hadn't stepped up. In fact, it was he who hadn't stepped up.

By stepping aside and placing the responsibility on the parishioners, rather than taking responsibility, and by prematurely and pessimistically pointing fingers rather than actually leading, the vicar lost his congregation. They understandably felt that if the vicar thought it was a lost cause, it was. Attendance and involvement tailed off to almost nothing, and the parish closed within six months of the unfortunate statements. Our words, as well as works, reveal our true beliefs.

Giving in to our fear

There's no doubt stepping up can be scary, whether it involves confronting the president of your company or your mother. Stepping up often means taking a risk, maybe not with your life, but perhaps with a job or a relationship. Worried about what might happen if we step up, we step aside instead and let someone else take the risk.

It's like that great commercial from the 1970s for Life cereal. Three young brothers are sitting at the breakfast table, wrestling with whether they should risk it and try a new cereal that's supposed to be good for you. They go back and forth: "I'm not gonna try it. You try it." Finally, the two older brothers get the idea to step aside. They push the bowl in front of their younger brother, Mikey, who "hates everything." To their shock, he starts devouring the cereal. "He likes it! Hey, Mikey!"

Frank Porter isn't planning on using his former protégé Arnold Bloom as a guinea pig, but he is stepping aside out of fear. Frank, fifty-nine, is an executive vice president, heading an important division in a consumer products company. He hired Arnold, forty-seven, two years ago to head his division's marketing arm. A brash, aggressive manager, Arnold shook up the marketing department. His energy gave the moribund staff a needed stimulus, and within eighteen months the transformation was reflected in the bottom line. But Arnold's abrasiveness earned him enemies in his own department and among his peers in other divisions and departments. Some of the other managers covertly complained to the executive committee and board. Frank knows Arnold's personality won't play well with the staid, conservative leadership team. While Frank would like to keep Arnold on board, he's afraid that if he goes to bat for him, he'll damage his own image with the board. Fearful of hurting his chances for further advancement, he decides to step aside and let Arnold defend himself.

STEPPING UP BY STANDING FIRM

The second U.S. Open was held at the Shinnecock Hills Golf Club on eastern Long Island in 1896. Sixteen-year-old John Shippen, a caddie at the club, entered the tournament. Shippen, whose father was a Baptist missionary at the nearby Shinnecock Indian reservation, was African American.

When some of the other players learned about Shippen, they threatened to withdraw rather than play with a black man. The lead official of the U.S. Golf Association at the time was Theodore Havemeyer, an executive with the American Sugar Company. Havemeyer heard the other players out, then told them they could do whatever they liked, play or not play, but Shippen would be in the field. John Shippen finished tied for fifth, seven strokes back.

Giving in to our anger

Finally, we step aside out of anger. Upset at someone, we decide to punish her through passive-aggressive behavior. Instead of confronting her directly, we harm her through inaction of some kind. This often comes out of conflicts over control and, as a result, is common among couples or pairs of coworkers who have equal status but are always vying for some kind of advantage. It's certainly a control issue that's driving Tom Waterburg to step aside.

Tom, fifty-two, has been working as a university administrator for more than twenty years, the last fifteen at the same state university. A year ago the university provost put Tom in charge of the search for a new head of development for the college he manages. The standout candidate was Mike Carver, thirty-nine, a well-connected attorney who had spent most of his time working as a fund-raiser for a political party. Tom was a bit annoyed when Mike was offered a salary equal to his own, despite Mike's being a subordinate. He grudgingly accepted the provost's rationales and hoped for the best. While Mike has been a successful fund-raiser, his work habits have been driving Tom crazy. Mike rarely comes in before ten thirty and is out to lunch by twelve thirty. Two hours later he returns to the office to make telephone calls and answer e-mails for a couple of hours. By four thirty he's gone for the day. A few weeks ago, Tom was called into the provost's office and told of an important project. The former leader of a large and controversial Asian nation was planning a visit to the campus to see his daughter, who's studying for her master's. Tom said that while he'd love to handle all the arrangements himself, he couldn't spare the time. Instead, he suggested Mike take charge. The provost, still enamored with Mike's pedigree, readily agreed. Tom is stepping aside knowing, or at least hoping, Mike will fail at an essential project requiring long hours of hard work.

We're capable of the worst . . . and the best

Stepping aside out of fear, as Frank Porter did, while unfortunate, is something to which most of us can relate. We can't be brave all the time. Even great heroes reach their limits . . . and the same is true of the rest of us.

And self-righteousness, while irksome, is also understandable. Everyone has an ego, and sometimes it gets the best of us. Doing the right thing doesn't always bring us acclaim from others, and as a result sometimes we provide it on our own or think we're entitled to take a break now and then.

It's stepping aside out of anger that's the most troubling to consider. It means setting someone else up for failure, knowingly putting someone else in harm's way. We don't like to think we're all capable of such behavior, but we are.

I was at Ground Zero on September 11, 2001, and for several days following. I witnessed firsthand the horrors human beings can inflict on others. We have the capability to be the most destructive, frightening force in nature. While there, I was blessed to be able to spend time offering assistance to those trying to rescue and then recover victims. That showed me that we human beings also have the potential to be the most loving, creative, life-giving forces in creation. The choice is ours.

DANGEROUS SAFARI

In the summer of 2001 my sons, John and Matt, and I decided to go on an environmental-learning safari to Africa. On our flight over, a series of fights broke out among the passengers. Fans of rival soccer teams were on board, and what started out as friendly ribbing turned ugly as the flight went on and more alcohol was consumed. Being stuck in a tightly packed enclosed cabin with drunken, rowdy brawlers was terrifying. I thought I should try to use my conflict-management skills since I lead workshops on the subject (although it's always easier to teach it than to live it). Fortunately, the skills came in handy. We landed intact and then spent two weeks as part of a small party camping deep in the African wilderness. Lions, hyenas, elephants, Cape buffalo, and other potentially dangerous animals visited our campsite every night. On what was thankfully an uneventful flight home, the boys and I went over our experiences. We all agreed the most frightening part of the trip was being stuck in a plane with other humans, not being surrounded by wild animals.

We have opportunities to make that choice every day, whether it's at home or in our workplace.

Philanthropic face-off

Aaron Brown, forty-six, is a wizard with numbers. With his diploma from one of America's leading undergraduate business schools, he could have gotten a job with any major accounting firm. But there's more to Aaron than just numbers. His parents, one a high school teacher and the other a social worker, instilled a tremendous dedication to public service in Aaron.

Rather than following the traditional path expected of accounting majors, Aaron went on to get his master's in public policy. At that point he took a job for one of Seattle's leading charitable foundations. He moved on to another agency after a few years and, in the next decade, climbed the ladder at the agency while earning his doctorate in nonprofit management. He earned a well-deserved reputation in the not-for-profit community for being a master at financial matters. That's why when the city decided to put together a multiagency task force, the high-powered and politically connected board chose him to serve as comptroller.

Aaron was dedicated to making sure every dollar was well spent and that as much money as possible was actually serving those in need. He did that by closely monitoring the spending of the agencies and groups hired by the task force to deliver services. Aaron never pulled punches, asked pointed questions, and wouldn't accept anything less than direct answers.

The staff members of two of the agencies bristled at the close scrutiny. The director of one of the agencies, Marianne Calovito, was particularly miffed. Never having had her expenditures questioned this closely before, she saw Aaron's efforts as contrary to the spirit of the task force. Marianne, the latest in a long line of family members who were fixtures on the Seattle charitable scene, had spent her entire career in the program, rather than the administrative side of not-for-profits. After six months of complaining to the board of the task force about Aaron's "antagonistic" attitude, Marianne finally convinced them to address the issue.

When called in to meet with the board about the dispute, Aaron listened closely and calmly as Marianne and others spoke. Then, when asked for his side of the issue, he stood up, thanked the board and everyone else for their time, told them he was sorry his efforts were misunderstood, and after a pregnant pause, nominated Marianne to take over as comptroller.

STEPPING UP BY PRESERVING JOBS

On December 11, 1995, the largest fire in Massachusetts in over a century destroyed the Malden Mills factory and instantly put three thousand people out of work. The company, known for producing Polartec, was one of the largest remaining employers in the economically deprived community of Lawrence. Most textile companies in the United States had already moved their factories from the Northeast and Mid-Atlantic to Southern states or overseas to save on labor costs, so it was assumed Malden Mills would now do the same. But Aaron Feuerstein, owner of the company, decided to step up by staying put.

Feuerstein, whose family had owned the company for three generations, decided to rebuild in Lawrence, rather than relocate. In addition, he paid all employees their full salaries and benefits for ninety days after the fire. Using the insurance settlement and investing additional money, Feuerstein rebuilt a state-of-the-art, environmentally and worker friendly factory. While admitting part of his motivation was to keep a family business alive, he also said he felt a responsibility to care for his employees. "I think it was a wise business decision," said Feuerstein, citing continued employee loyalty and dedication, "but that isn't why I did it. I did it because it was the right thing to do."

Living on the edge

Perhaps the only person less qualified to be a comptroller than Marianne is Stephanie Wendhover, a single woman who works as a fashion editor for a women's magazine. Short, with aquiline features and closely cropped black hair, Stephanie is a regular on the cultural circuit, attending gallery openings, concerts, and theatrical performances.

Stephanie attended a prestigious all-girls school in New England, where she majored in art history. Drawing on alumni contacts and family connections, she landed a position as an editorial assistant at a Southern lifestyle magazine. She quickly climbed the editorial ladder, owing to her skill as a networker as well as her eye for cutting-edge cultural trends. As time passed, Stephanie's approval of a new designer, a young artist, or a newly opened club became an imprimatur for a group of young media elites. When quizzed about her taste, Stephanie always explained that she was attracted to edginess: clothes, art, or places that took risks and didn't care about conventional or mainstream attitudes.

While her status as a tastemaker and trendsetter was rewarding, Stephanie was beginning to feel that her career was reaching a dead end. The upper editors at her magazine were older, with corporate rather than cultural connections, and unlikely to be leaving anytime soon. Her peers in similar positions on other magazines didn't earn any more than she did, and her magazine provided greater personal exposure than would any of the alternatives. This lack of any real avenues for advancement was the reason she listened closely when approached by a group interested in launching a new venture.

A young art-critic friend of Stephanie's, Simon Hastings, explained to her that a magazine entrepreneur who had recently sold his innovative technology title to a major publishing company was working on a new media concept. He wanted to combine features of magazines, Web sites, and television shows into a cultural program designed for podcasting and satellite radio. His idea was to combine cutting-edge technologies with cutting-edge culture. Simon told Stephanie that start-up money wasn't a problem, and she could have double her current salary. However, the entrepreneur was only willing to commit to a two-year test. If the venture wasn't breaking even by then, he would pull the plug. Simon, as committed to cutting-edge culture as Stephanie, saw this as the perfect opportunity for her to not only break out of magazines, but to really stake a place for herself in the world of cultural media.

Stephanie told Simon she'd think about it and get back to him in a couple of days. Over dinner and drinks that night with friends, she discussed it further. The next morning she had breakfast with some other friends and felt them out about it. By late the next afternoon she had decided. Stephanie called Simon and explained she simply couldn't take the risk financially and career-wise. If things didn't work out, it would set her career back. However, she said she would be eager to speak to the entrepreneur and explain that Simon himself was actually the perfect person to head up the venture.

STEPPING UP FOR THE ILL

Tom Watson was in contention at the 1980 U.S. Open held at Baltusrol, in Springfield, New Jersey. A couple of hours before he was scheduled to tee off for his final round, an official came over to him. He explained to Watson that a member of the club, Dr. William A. Tansey, wanted very much to see him. When Watson asked where the member was, the official explained Tansey was a few minutes' drive away at his home. Tansey was bedridden with terminal cancer. Without hesitation Watson went to visit Tansey and spent about half an hour chatting with the dying man.

Later that day Watson was asked why he would take the time to visit when he could have been preparing for the last round of the Open. Watson looked puzzled: "You can't take golf so seriously you rule out what is the human thing to do."

Staying on the bench

I can understand Stephanie's hesitancy. My father was career military, and as a result our family moved around a great deal when I was growing up. When my father retired from the Marine Corps, and we finally settled down in Gainesville, Florida, I was just about to enter my first year of high school. I had been an overweight kid from late elementary through high school, but in our second summer in Gainesville I shot up four inches and, thanks to working at an outdoor construction job, in ninety-five-degree heat, lost twenty pounds. When I showed up for my sophomore year of high school, I looked and felt like a different person. Having been picked on a great deal when I was younger due to my weight, I was determined to start off on the right track in this new school.

I soon learned the two secrets to social success at the school were being able to dance and being a member of the school's state-champion-caliber football program. I was already a good dancer, but I had never played football before. Determined as I was to fit in, I didn't let that stand in my way. I worked hard in tryouts and made the junior varsity team. But once having made the team, I had a change of heart.

Even to this day I'm not sure why, but at the end of our second game, when the coach came up to me and told me to go into the game, I instead suggested he send in another of the guys who'd been warming the bench with me. The coach looked at me quizzically, then shifted his attention to the other player. For the rest of the season I became persona non grata to the coach and rode the bench. Then, in the fourth quarter of our last game, the coach announced that everyone who hadn't played yet that year should gather around him so he could get everyone in the game. By this point I was ready to step up and play, but the clock wound down and I never actually got in a game. The next year I tried out for baseball instead and fared much better.

What would it look like if we stepped up?

I don't know what would have happened had the Clinton administration intervened in Rwanda, or if Richard Nixon had stepped up and taken responsibility for the Watergate break-in, but I can guess what would have happened had the rest of us discussed in this chapter stepped up rather than stepped aside.

Diane Ferguson thought she was doing the right thing by stepping aside and putting her husband Philip's educational plans ahead of her own. Actually, what she saw as self-sacrifice diminished her in Philip's eyes. Diane played the martyr and ended up suffering a martyr's fate. If she'd stepped up for herself and worked with Philip in developing a plan so they could both share in the sacrifice and its fruits, their relationship may have flourished rather than falling apart. That's not for certain, but at least Diane would have been in a healthier place emotionally and psychologically as well as financially.

STEPPING UP BY OFFERING THANKS

In 1938, Marjorie Courtenay-Latimer was the curator of fish and fossils for a small museum on the coast of South Africa. For years she had been receiving specimens for the museum from helpful local fishermen. One day she received a telephone call from two trawler men, Irvin and Johnson, who had been helpful. They told her they had a new catch for her to look through if she was interested. Courtenay-Latimer already had more specimens than she needed for an upcoming display, and since it was just a few days before her Christmas holiday, she was tempted to turn down the invitation. But then she remembered how helpful the two men had been to her and realized this would be a good excuse to stop by, thank them for their help over the years, and wish them both a happy Christmas. So she stepped up and went for a visit.

Once she arrived at the boat and had finished giving her season's greetings to the trawler men, Courtenay-Latimer began picking through their catch. Her eye was attracted to a strange-looking, five-foot-long fish. It had four limblike fins and what looked like a tail. The more she studied it the more she thought they might have found something remarkable. They had. Courtenay-Latimer was looking at the first discovery of a coelacanth-like fish that had originated about 400 million years ago and had somehow survived. The discovery sent shock waves throughout the world of science. Five years later another specimen was discovered. By then the species had been named *Latimeria chalumnae,* after Courtenay-Latimer.

There's no guarantee Frank Porter could have saved Arnold Bloom's job and still maintained his own position in the company. But had he stepped up, he could both have defended a productive, effective subordinate whose value to the company was unquestioned and coached that subordinate to keep from making the same mistakes in the future. Frank had a chance to make a difference for the company, for Arnold's future, and, I think, for himself as well. It would have been far better for his soul in the short term, and perhaps for his future at the company in the long term, if he'd risen to the occasion and defended his protégé.

Tom Waterburg could have stepped up by having a talk with Mike Carver about his work habits. And whether or not that conversation made a difference, Tom could also have stepped up for the university by either taking on the important assignment himself, or at least insuring that whoever did take the job was in a position to succeed. Setting Mike up for failure may satisfy Tom's need for revenge, but it won't really do anything positive. Mike will be hurt, the university will be hurt, and Tom will be hurt by giving in to his basest impulses.

Like Tom, Aaron Brown could have stepped up rather than

step aside for his critic Marianne Calovito. Aaron could have been a bit more concerned with people's feelings while still giving financial efficiency the priority. Sometimes all it takes is to hear people out and give them a chance to make their case. Perhaps if he then explained his motivations, everyone could have come together in some way. But even if that didn't happen, Aaron could have stepped up by helping the task force through a transition, rather than leaving in a lurch and dumping the matter on his chief critic's lap. If he truly wanted to do what was best for the task force, he could have stepped up and put its interest ahead of his own ego, at least temporarily.

Stephanie Wendhover could have stepped up by taking a chance. No one looks back on their lives from the perspective of old age and says, "I should have taken fewer chances." The comment is always "I wish I took more risks." By stepping up and embracing change and risk, Stephanie could have brought her external life in greater sync with her inner life. All our lives are finite, and as a result our opportunities are finite. Each chance to reach out, to grow, to expand our hearts or our minds, is a precious opportunity. It may not be our last chance, but that particular circumstance will never come again. And so what if we do fail? We only end up where we started!

I wish I had known that when I was on the sidelines back in high school. Having unaccountably turned down the chance to play in a game, I passed up what I thought was the only opportunity I would have in my entire life to play in an organized football game. Did it destroy my life? Obviously not. In the great scheme of my life it was only a little thing. But the point is that it never came again. Because I stepped aside rather than stepping up, I lost something small but still precious. Every time we skip a child's recital, pass up a drink with an old friend, cancel a stroll with a loved one, or even just give up a chance to stop and admire a sunset, we diminish ourselves. It may only be by a little. But those tiny pieces add up over a lifetime. Don't step aside. Assume responsibility for yourself first, then for others, for your world, and above all, for the difference you want to make by making decisions that matter.

If I am not for myself, who will be for me? And if I am only for myself, what am I? And if not now—when?

—Hillel

4

Stepping Back

I am the center of the world, but the control panel seems to be somewhere else.

—Mason Cooley

You're not the only one who can, or needs to, step up. Everyone wants to experience meaning in his or her life, and all of us are confronted with opportunities in which we can step up and satisfy that desire. Yet at times, rather than helping or letting others step up, we instead step back and block them.

Stepping back is preventing someone else from taking action in a situation we know needs to be addressed. Let's say your adolescent daughter receives a new winter coat as a Christmas present. She tells you that she'd like to give her old coat to a schoolmate who's commented on how much she loves the coat and who doesn't seem to have a good winter coat. You'd prefer your daughter hold on to the old coat to use when playing in the snow. Besides, you explain to your daughter, offering the coat might embarrass the other girl and her parents. Odds are that rationalization works and you successfully block your daughter from stepping up and passing along her old coat.

It has become common for us to use the phrase *step back* to refer to a pause; a time-out for thought or analysis. But stepping back isn't passive at all. Just because you stop, doesn't

113

mean the world stops. You aren't the center of the universe. When you step back, you often prevent others from moving forward; you keep the situation from being addressed; you stop others from stepping up. If you truly need a time-out, you should say you're stepping aside, instead of stepping back, implying that you're giving others a chance to keep on moving.*

Mourners commonly suffer from this sort of self-centered attitude. Because they've been hit with such a traumatic blow, they become frozen with grief. People close to them offer comfort and support. After a brief respite, the nonmourners move on with their lives. The mourners, meanwhile, can't understand. How can those people just go back to work or go on with their lives as they did before? they wonder. Mourners' self-centeredness is excusable: we all need a space of our own and some time to heal. But no one is entitled to block other people from moving forward.

When I was studying in Jerusalem years ago, I went on a tour of Hezekiah's tunnel. This is an underground tunnel one-third of a mile long, about three feet wide, and in places less than five feet high, believed to have been dug in the time of King Hezekiah (about 701 BCE) to provide a hidden water source if the city was under siege. Obviously, tourists can only progress slowly and one at a time. I was at the end of the group. Ahead of me were some active seniors, part of a group I was leading, and ahead of them, at the front of the line, was a pack

---

*It may seem like a minor matter, but I think semantics like this can be important. I think we should be just as careful in choosing our words in the workplace as we are at home. You think about how to say things to your loved ones—or at least you should—and you should also think about how to say things to your workplace peers, subordinates, and superiors.

of teens. The teenagers were laughing and goofing around, as teenagers are apt to do. But every time they'd stop short, the seniors behind them were blocked and became more and more agitated and claustrophobic. Rather than stepping up for a thrilling adventure, the active seniors found the trip through the tunnel a nightmare.

I'm not sure why those teens stepped back and blocked Hezekiah's tunnel, but the core reason why most of us step back at work and in our personal lives is simple: ego. Stepping back is always about putting ourselves first. Generally, we do that in one of three ways: giving in to a sense of entitlement; struggling to retain control; or putting the means to a goal above the goal itself.

STEPPING BACK INTO THE COLOR LINE

Cap Anson was a star player-manager of the Chicago Whitestockings whose skills earned him a spot in the Hall of Fame. But he's also responsible for segregating baseball.

On July 14, 1887, Anson intimidated the Newark Little Giants into pulling their African American battery of pitcher George Stovey and catcher Fleet Walker from an exhibition game by threatening to pull the Whitestockings off the field. Anson was, in effect, stepping back and blocking Stovey and Walker. By the end of that year, teams were copying Anson's threat, leading the International League to institute an unofficial color line that was subsequently embraced by the National and American leagues until Jackie Robinson and Branch Rickey of the Brooklyn Dodgers broke it in 1947.

What's not often remembered, however, is that someone did try to step up and stop Anson. In 1883, Anson had tried the same threat in a game with Toledo, for whom Fleet Walker was then playing. But Charley Morton, manager of Toledo, stepped up by stepping on Anson. Even though he'd actually had no intention of having Walker in the lineup that day because he needed to rest an injury, Morton called Anson's bluff and said either Walker would be behind the plate or there wouldn't be any game. Anson backed down.

If more people had had Charley Morton's strength of character and had stepped up rather than stepping back, baseball might have avoided a blot on its history.

A SENSE OF ENTITLEMENT

Sometimes we step back to block someone else from getting something to which we feel entitled. I'm not talking about honest, overt, head-to-head competition. That's healthy. I'm referring to covert sabotage or the undermining of someone through faint praise, or a backstabbing campaign of whispers and innuendo. I believe any time we start thinking we deserve or are entitled to something, we're heading down a potentially damaging psychological path . . . damaging to ourselves as well as others.

I remember a particularly telling moment in the Clint Eastwood film *Unforgiven*. Will Munny, played by Eastwood, is a hired gun looking for some kind of redemption. Little Bill Daggett, played by Gene Hackman, is a former gunfighter now trying to settle down as a sheriff. The moral ambiguity of both characters comes to a head when Munny guns down Little Bill in the film's climax. As Little Bill lies dying, he looks up to Munny and says, "I don't deserve this. To die like this. I was building a house." Munny looks down and says, "Deserve's got nothing to do with it." He's right. Neither deserve nor entitlement have anything to do with it for any of us.

A most infamous instance of stepping back surrounded the 1800 U.S. presidential election. Thomas Jefferson chose Aaron Burr to be his partner on the Democratic-Republican ticket. At that time presidential electors were chosen by state legislatures rather than voters, and Burr's home state of New York was critical to the election.

While it was understood by all that Jefferson was running for president and Burr for vice president, the Constitution at that time awarded the vice presidency to whoever had the second-most votes. In a surprise, Jefferson and Burr received the exact same number of votes in the electoral college, throwing the election into the House of Representatives.

Burr, rather than stepping aside as he'd promised to be the vice president, decided to instead step back and block Jefferson's election in an effort to win the presidency himself. He started courting his former allies in the Federalist party. It took thirty-five ballots over three days for the election finally to be decided in Jefferson's favor.

Liza Roberts will never be as infamous as Aaron Burr, but she stepped back as well. A thirty-two-year-old, lanky blonde with a dazzling personality, Liza was the top-selling regional salesperson for a major manufacturer of optics equipment. This year, however, Darren Truman, twenty-nine, was on pace to be the top performer of the sales staff. Liza, convinced Darren had benefited unfairly from the economic boom of one city in his region, was angry she might miss out on the $5,000 bonus and extra week of vacation awarded annually to the top salesperson. During the sales meeting prior to the launching of the company's newest products, the national sales manager and the director of marketing solicited ideas from the staff. Liza had a couple of suggestions, but spent most of her time and energy throwing subtle roadblocks in the way of Darren's idea.

THE NEED FOR CONTROL

Sometimes we step back to block someone else from taking away our control. Unlike blocking out of a sense of entitlement, blocking because we need to assert control usually comes from the best of motivations. We think we're helping someone out because we feel we know better or can do something better. Even though we're blocking someone, we tell ourselves we're doing it to protect them from themselves. Psychiatrist Thomas Szasz has explained this by noting, "We often speak of love when we really should be speaking of the drive to dominate or to master, so as to confirm ourselves as active agents, in control of our own destinies and worthy of respect from others."

Don't get me wrong: at times stepping back is clearly beneficial—for instance, when you take away the car keys from a friend who has had too much to drink, or when you keep a child from touching a red-hot stove. But most times, stepping back to control, whatever the motivation, isn't so clearly the right thing.

It is a conquest when we can lift ourselves above the annoyances of circumstances over which we have no control; but it is a greater victory when we can make those circumstances our helpers—when we can appreciate the good there is in them. It has often seemed to me as if Life stood beside me, looking me in the face, and saying, "Child, you must learn to like me in the form in which you see me, before I can offer myself to you in any other aspect."

—Lucy Larcom

Right after the attacks of September 11, 2001, my eldest son, John, who was a junior in high school, told me he wanted to sign up for the U.S. Marine Corps Reserve. I know he was inspired by the need to somehow respond to the attack, as well as out of admiration for my father. I thought he was acting impulsively. I felt that, until he turned eighteen, I had the parental authority to step back and block him from signing up. I told him that after he graduated high school and turned eighteen, he could make the decision on his own. Three years later he was a sophomore in college. He telephoned to tell me he was planning to join the Marine Corps Reserve. I gave him my blessings. Was I right to step back when he first tried to sign up? I think so. Was I right not to step back three years later? I think so. But I'm far from certain.

Just as I had tried to protect my son, Tina Iverson's husband tried to protect her. Tina, fifty-four, has always felt the need to serve. That's one reason why Tina became a physician. But after more than twenty years in private practice as a gynecologist, she feels the need to do more than just help her patients. Right after New Year's she sat down for a heart-to-heart talk with her husband, Sandy, fifty-seven, an orthopedic surgeon. Sandy, a burly former college athlete, already knew about Tina's need to serve, but he didn't realize how it had grown. Tina explained that she wanted to give up her practice and begin working with Doctors Without Borders (Médecins Sans Frontières). Fluent in both French and Spanish as well as English, thanks to her father having been in the diplomatic service, and experienced at providing care to women, Tina knew she was a prime candidate. Sandy, however, hates the idea. Not only would she be leaving him behind with their two sons, one a college sophomore and the other in his last year of high school, but she would likely be going to dangerous parts of the world. He's afraid he won't be able to protect her. Sandy has spent the past two years using every tool at his disposal—guilt, fear, anger—to block Tina from stepping up.

———

Time in the hand is not control of time,

Nor shattered fragments of an instrument

A proof against the wind; the wind will rise,

We can only close the shutters.

—Adrienne Rich

———

PUTTING MEANS ABOVE ENDS

Finally, in some instances we step back to block action so our roles in some process (and by extension, we personally) retain importance. When you're part of an organization or system, whether it's a bureaucracy or a family, your role becomes symbolic of you. If you're the one who always hangs the garland on the tree, you come to believe it's not a proper Christmas until that garland is hung. And if you're the one who's responsible for a particular step in a bureaucratic procedure, you'll consider that the essential step that can never be ignored. We often lose sight of what's important by putting more value on the means than the end. The goal gets obscured by the process and procedure. The philosopher Eric Hoffer has observed, "We have perhaps a natural fear of ends. We would rather be always on the way than arrive. Given the means, we hang on to them and often forget the ends."

Sometimes this self-centered view of procedure is so over-the-top it can be amusing. I went on a tour of the Palace of Westminster in London, where Parliament sits, led by a clerk. The clerks are generally retired military personnel, and each has a particular role. The clerk who led my tour was in charge of the message center. Needless to say the group spent a great deal of time by the message board being regaled with tales of how essential it is to the operation of the government.

"SORRY, GET YOUR OWN AMMO"

In 1879 a British military column, having invaded Zululand, was camped by a mountain called Isandlwana. Because of the size of the force and the difficult terrain, the British didn't fortify their camp, but, instead, sent out extended lines and picket posts. A massive Zulu army appeared suddenly and attacked the camp. The British had just begun using breech-loading rifles and were concerned with the cost of using too much ammunition. Each company had its own quartermaster who was in charge of distributing ammunition according to strict rules and regulations. As the battle raged and the troops began to run out of ammunition, they ran back to get more from the closest source. But the quartermasters refused to give ammunition to anyone who wasn't from their own unit. The Zulu army overwhelmed the British, taking no prisoners and leaving fourteen hundred dead redcoats . . . along with lots of unused ammunition.

All too often, however, this self-centered focus on means rather than ends leads to financial loss and possibly real human hardship. Jack Turley, forty-nine, is regional manager of a chain of home improvement stores. Having worked his way up from salesclerk to department manager to store manager to regional manager, Jack is a dedicated company man with hopes of moving up into the national management soon. Early one Friday morning he received a call on his cell phone from the manager of one of the larger stores in his region. The manager had just seen an early projection that a hurricane building off the East Coast was potentially heading in his direction. He knew that if the hurricane continued on its present course there'd soon be a rush on plywood, batteries, and all sorts of emergency supplies. He was calling Jack to see if he could get backup inventory from some of the other stores in the region that weren't in the hurricane's path. He was already running low on some products and was afraid he'd soon have to send people away empty-handed. Jack patiently explained to him that product couldn't be shipped from store to store. For the company to keep constant track of its inventory—one of its keys to profitability—product needed to travel to and from the distribution center. Jack explained the manager needed to call in his request to the distribution center, which would have it ready . . . on Monday.

The three hermits

Though obsessive or excessive adherence to process over results is most often associated with bureaucracy, it threatens to infect all of us. And no matter how noble our motivation, it is likely misguided. One of my favorite examples is a wonderful story written by Leo Tolstoy in his book *Twenty-three Tales.*

"COUNSELING" FOR HAVING STEPPED UP

U.S. Navy helicopter pilots Lieutenant Matt Udkow and Lieutenant David Shand had finished delivering supplies to sites in Mississippi and were on the way back to their base in Pensacola, Florida, when they overheard Coast Guard radio calls asking for helicopters to help rescue people stranded by Hurricane Katrina in New Orleans. Unable to get in touch with their base for permission, Udkow and Shand took the initiative and flew their H-3 helicopters to New Orleans and within minutes were rescuing dozens of people off rooftops. After landing to refuel in New Orleans, they received permission to continue with the rescue missions. By the end of the day they had rescued 110 victims. But when they arrived back in Pensacola later that evening, both were "counseled" about the importance of supply missions. I'm not sure the navy would consider it stepping back, but Udkow was then reassigned to take charge of a temporary kennel in Pensacola for pets of military personnel displaced by Katrina.

A bishop is taking an ocean journey from his home city to visit a famous monastery. One afternoon he sees a crowd on the boat deck listening closely to one of the crew. The bishop casually walks over to listen. The crewman, seeing the bishop, repeats his story. He points to a small island off in the distance and explains that one day when he was out fishing, he was caught in a storm and his boat washed up there. He discovered three hermits living on the island, who took care of him and helped repair his boat. The crewman said the hermits told him they were living there for the salvation of their souls.

The bishop, fascinated by the story, asks the boat's captain if they can take a brief detour to the island so he might visit the hermits. The captain agrees, and the next morning a ship's boat rows the bishop to the island. When he lands, he quickly meets the three hermits. They are old men with long beards who seem uncomfortable speaking, but who are clearly seeking spiritual enlightenment.

The bishop tells them he'd like to help. He asks how they pray. The youngest and tallest of the hermits explains that they simply gaze upward and say, "Three are ye, three are we, have mercy upon us." The bishop smiles and tells them that while they're clearly godly men, they need to learn to pray as commanded in the Holy Scriptures.

Throughout the day the bishop lectured the hermits on Scripture and told them the importance of learning the Lord's Prayer. Over and over he drilled the hermits. It took hours of repetition and patience, but finally it seemed as if the hermits had memorized the Lord's Prayer. As the sun set, the bishop, feeling he had accomplished much good, set off back to the ship.

On the trip back to the ship, and once on board, the bishop could hear the hermits reciting the prayer. And as the ship got under way, he could still faintly hear the prayers of the hermits. Finally, the sound grew quieter and eventually vanished as the ship sailed away. The bishop, pleased with his day's efforts, said a quick prayer, thanking God for having sent him to teach the three men.

Just as he was about to go belowdecks to his cabin, the bishop saw a faint glow in the distance. It was moving toward the boat at a high speed. At first he couldn't make it out. But as it drew closer, it took form. To the bishop's amazement and the shock of the crew still on deck, they saw the source of the glow. The three hermits, gray hair and beards shining, were running on the water toward them at an incredible speed. In stunned amazement the bishop and the crew stood transfixed as the hermits came near the boat.

The youngest of the three looked up at the bishop and began to speak. "We have forgotten your teaching, servant of God. As long as we kept repeating it, we remembered, but when we stopped saying it for a time, a word dropped out, and now it has all gone to pieces. We can remember nothing of it. Teach us again." The bishop crossed himself, then responded, "Your own prayer will reach the Lord, men of God. It is not for me to teach you. Pray for us sinners."

Stepping back isn't limited to bishops visiting hermits. Each of us has the potential to step back in both our work and personal lives.

From golden boy to problem child

Simon Kent, forty-two, brought a reputation for effectiveness with him to his current employer. Before landing his job as leader of an investigative news team for an influential business magazine, Simon was the metropolitan editor for a newspaper in a major European capital. A reedy man with a shaved head and a perpetually disheveled appearance, Simon projects impatience and aggression. Even his biggest detractors admit those traits probably add to his effectiveness. But they've also led to his current problems.

———

When you are praying, do not heap up empty phrases as the Gentiles do; for they think that they will be heard of their many words. Do not be like them, for your Father knows what you need before you ask him.

—Matthew 6:7–8

———

When he was first hired, Simon was told the culture of the magazine he was joining was unique. While bottom-line effectiveness was vital, so was the ability to become part of a collaborative management team. The president of the company that owned the magazine was a devotee of corporate team building. Unique among its competitors, the publication was viewed as an excellent place to work, and the holding company itself was always looking to promote from within.

Within the first six months of his arrival, Simon made a splash. His investigative team dug up a story that rocked a major industry, gathered national notice from the mainstream press, and earned a series of journalism awards. Subscriptions and newsstand sales jumped, and sales staff reported positive comments from prospective advertisers. Taking his usual aggressive approach, Simon decided to parlay his early success into more power and a bigger paycheck. At a hastily called meeting with the publisher and president, he pushed for a larger staff, a bigger budget, and 20 percent hike in his compensation package. While both the publisher and company president were duly complimentary about his work and enthusiastic about his future at the magazine and the company, they said he was jumping the gun. They'd be happy, maybe even eager, to revisit the conversation in another six months.

That wasn't good enough for Simon. While he voiced acceptance, if not happiness, with the decision, his impatience began to get the better of him. His investigative team continued its hard work, albeit without another spectacular success. But Simon, confident his triumph had made him a company star, began acting like a prima donna. Angry at not receiving what he considered just rewards, he began stepping back. During weekly editorial-board meetings he offered litanies of criticisms without any accompanying compliments. Whenever asked to help with magazine or companywide initiatives, he'd brush off the requests. At a quarterly meeting of the company's senior management, he did his best to derail two projects that he thought might drain off resources he could potentially use, and which might better position two of his peers for advancement. His attitude and body language demonstrated not just cockiness, but almost animosity.

After another six months of this stepping back, he'd gone

from "golden boy" to "problem child" in his publisher's eyes. The publisher, tempted to push for his termination, was placated by the president's intervention. At Simon's subsequent performance review the president did most of the talking. He reminded Simon of the value the company placed on collaboration and teamwork. Simon was told that despite his successes his future with the company was now questionable due to his attitude.

LOSING SIGHT OF THE BIG PICTURE

It's not just individuals who can step back; organizations and systems sometimes block progress. In 1970, Xerox established its Palo Alto Research Center (PARC) as a research division. Under some astute visionary leadership, PARC soon became a hotbed of innovation. In effect, PARC invented the personal computer.

Their system, called the Alto, included a mouse, computer-generated color graphics, a "what you see is what you get" text editor, a graphic-page description language (precursor to Post-Script), Ethernet, object-oriented programming, an integrated development environment, and laser printing. In addition, Xerox developed the graphical user interface—the desktop environment—eventually popularized by the Apple Macintosh. Xerox had the entire future of the personal computing industry in its hands . . . and dropped the mouse. Why?

While there are many individual theories, most business observers concur that the Xerox culture viewed innovations strictly as to how they would impact its photocopier business. The company stepped back and blocked the wider development and marketing of these new technologies out of fear they would reduce the number of photocopies offices would be making.

Holding on to the veto

Cheryl Wang, thirty-nine, is devoted to her father's memory. Along with her older sister, Karen, forty-four, Cheryl has been helping their mother, Margaret, manage the considerable nest egg their deceased father, a successful real estate developer, left behind. The father, a stickler for keeping things "in the family," had constructed an elaborate process for decision making. Cheryl, an attorney, and Karen, a physician, both have seats on an executive committee that also includes Karen's husband, an accountant, Margaret herself, and one outsider: the late father's former personal attorney. Cheryl, Margaret, and Karen are the only members with votes. In an effort that he thought would foster long-term family unity, the father stipulated that all decisions needed to be unanimous, and that everyone must vote in person.

For years the process worked fine. The estate was well managed and few decisions were actually required. The handful of votes that needed to take place were easily arranged around events when the family would be together anyway, such as holidays and birthdays. But as Margaret has grown older, the process has created problems. For her to get the most effective use of the estate's assets, there will need to be adjustments to the portfolio requiring more hands-on management. In addition, Margaret would now like to move from the Midwestern suburb in which they all currently live to the Sun Belt. That would make in-person voting difficult.

Karen, with the support of her husband, suggests they vote to amend the estate's rules either so that only two votes are required, or that voting can take place over a long distance. She, with the support of her husband and Margaret, argues that their father would never have wanted his rules to stand in the way of his wife's quality of life. The father's former attorney agrees. Cheryl, while not minimizing the issues, is hesitant to change the rules.

Cheryl argues that respect for the structure of the estate is the equivalent of respect for their father. As gently as possible she raises the potential problems of having majority rather than unanimous decisions. She also suggests that requiring in-person voting might be a way of forcing important stability on the estate. Seeing her arguments aren't working, Cheryl in frustration points out that, in effect, she has a veto over any changes. Ironically, her comments only antagonize her sister and sadden her mother, creating the very disunity her father's rules were designed to avoid.

Choosing someone's path for her

I know something about that kind of irony. A couple of years ago I faced a similar situation. A friend of mine was participating in regular self-help seminars that appeal to many single adults across the country. These seminars provide great support both during the large weekend sessions and also at the smaller group meetings held during the week.

I had a couple of problems with my friend's choice. First, I don't believe these types of short-term, intensive New Age events offer lasting spiritual development. I think that while they may provide a brief spiritual high, they can leave attendees even more bereft of spiritual sustenance than they were beforehand. They're sort of like a spiritual candy bar. If you eat that candy bar when you're tired, you'll get a quick sugar-induced energy rush. But as soon as it wears off, you're even more tired than before. And second, like some other churches and religious institutions, these seminars are often more about making money and building a business than about prolonging and sustaining the spiritual growth of their participants.

Drawing on my education about psychological and spiritual matters, plus my pastoral adviser experience, I encouraged—perhaps even bullied—my friend into giving up the seminars. Even though I think my objections to this kind of group are valid, I was wrong to stop my friend from attending. An old Buddhist proverb advises, "Better your own dharma [path] poorly done than someone else's dharma." I should have heeded those wise words. I may have kept a friend from finding and developing her own spiritual path.

What would it look like if we stepped up?

Let's go back to the individuals I've discussed in this chapter and see what it would have looked like had we all stepped up rather than stepping back.

Liza Roberts need not have spent so much time and energy throwing roadblocks in the path of her competitor Darren. She could have concentrated more on developing and promoting her own projects. In addition, Liza could have framed any legitimate points about Darren's ideas as suggestions that might provide a better chance for success. By putting the company's needs first, she would have improved the company's long-term position as well as her own.

STEPPING UP BY SHOWING SUPPORT

Wisconsin senator Robert M. La Follette was one of America's most impassioned progressives. He never hesitated to step up and vote his conscience, whatever the popular sentiment of the time. In April 1917 he spoke out against American entry into World War One. La Follette voted against the declaration of war and against conscription. Both votes were unpopular. In fact, some of La Follette's colleagues were so outraged by his antiwar stance that there were demands he be expelled from the Senate.

On the day a measure to expel La Follette was scheduled to be debated, he entered the chamber alone. Most senators ignored him. However, Pennsylvania's Boies Penrose, a Republican leader, strode right up to him. Penrose was one of the Senate's most conservative members and disagreed with the liberal La Follette on almost every issue. But Penrose hated hypocrisy and admired courage. Penrose put his arm around La Follette's shoulders and escorted him all the way down the center aisle to his seat. All the senators who had consciously been ignoring La Follette couldn't ignore such a blatant show of support from Penrose. The motion to expel La Follette was never brought to the floor.

Rather than using every way he could think of to prevent his wife, Tina, from joining Doctors Without Borders, Sandy Iverson could have tried to help her achieve her goal. There would have been nothing wrong with his raising his concerns and seeing if they could find some way for those to be adequately addressed while still giving her a chance to serve in a way she'd find satisfying. But in the final analysis, to step up he needs to help her step up too.

Jack Turley, the regional manager of home improvement stores, didn't need to stick so closely to procedures. Stepping up would have meant supporting the store manager to try to prepare for an emergency in every way possible. Bending the rules, even for just a day or two, would have helped empower his manager, provided positive lessons for other managers, boosted the company's image, and not incidentally, improved its bottom line by generating added sales. Taking the responsibility to bend the rules would have been a powerful way for him to step up.

Aggressiveness and impatience could just as easily have been harnessed to stepping up as stepping back, had Simon Kent chosen to do so. Rather than being aggressive and impatient in the pursuit of personal reward, he could have stepped up by applying that drive to all the company's goals, not just his own. Had Simon shown the same concern with the company's other initiatives and been aggressive in his collaborative efforts, he would probably have received just the rewards he desired, albeit after a brief delay.

Cheryl Wang's devotion to her father would better have been served by honoring his goals rather than the means he'd created to reach those goals. Instead of standing in the way of changes to the estate rules that would have improved her mother's quality of life, she could have stepped up by trying to develop some compromise. For instance, she might have suggested that only certain types of decisions required unanimous votes, or that meetings also be held at her mother's future home. By stepping up and showing she was also focused on the goal, she could have avoided family strains.

Finally, I could certainly have done a better job in dealing with my friend's personal development search. Rather than blocking her from following her own path, I could have stepped up and given her the freedom of individual exploration to which we're all entitled. I could have stepped up for myself as well by being truer to my own beliefs by treating her as I'd wish to be treated, even if I disagreed with her chosen path: "So in everything, do to others what you would have them do to you, for this sums up the law and the prophets" (Matthew 7:12). Would that have resulted in the end of a friendship? I don't know. It might have—at least in the short term. But it might also have resulted in our relationship being stronger long term.

Stepping up is all about doing the right thing, the loving thing. It's not about doing the easiest or the most pleasurable thing. Besides heeding the advice from Matthew, I could have listened to Michel de Montaigne, who wrote, "Not being able to control events, I control myself; and I adapt myself to them, if they do not adapt themselves to me." Rather than stepping back to try to control things that are really beyond our control, you and I need to take charge of ourselves and step up and do what we can.

STEPPING UP BY STEPPING BACK

In January 1986 the National Aeronautics and Space Administration was under fire. The upcoming space shuttle launch had repeatedly been delayed. And with the presence of America's first "teacher in space," Christa McAuliffe, on the crew, the media attention was enormous. Finally, on January 28, *Challenger* lifted off, only to explode seventy-three seconds later, killing all seven crew members.

Investigations later revealed O-ring seals in the solid-rocket boosters of the shuttle had failed, and that the failure and subsequent disaster, far from unexpected, had been predicted. Two engineers at Morton Thiokol, Roger M. Boisloly and Allan McDonald, and one at NASA, senior analyst Richard C. Cook, had done their best to step back and block the upcoming launch, fearing that cold temperatures would lead to catastrophic O-ring failure. While they were, in the end, unable to prevent the disaster, they and the other individuals who braved institutional resistance stepped up.

5

Stepping on
Someone Else

The three hardest tasks in the world are neither physical feats nor intellectual achieve-
ments, but moral acts: to return love for hate,
to include the excluded, and to say, "I was
wrong."

—Sydney J. Harris

B reak the cycle. Instead of paying back an affront, insult, or
attack by stepping on someone else, step up. Instead of
looking to take advantage of another's weakness, step up. All
of us are guilty of attacking others in one way or another. We
wouldn't be human if we didn't. But we are all also capable of
transcending this natural urge for revenge or competitive advantage, thus opening the door for real personal and spiritual
growth.

Stepping on someone else means using someone else's situation for your advantage, usually by attacking them somehow.
It could be as revenge for their having stepped on you in the
past. Or it could be a way for you to "beat" them in some kind
of competition, real or imagined. You'd think such contentious

actions would only come after a great deal of thought. Actually, the reverse is usually the case.

Let's say you're waiting on line at the Department of Motor Vehicles. You've lots of other things to do and your frustration is growing in direct proportion to the size of the line and the length of time you're waiting. Finally, you're second in line. The person in front of you drops the cell phone she's been talking on, to your increasing annoyance. As she bends down to look for it, one of the clerks waves for the next person in line. Seizing the opportunity, you nimbly glide by the distracted woman in front of you and approach the waiting clerk.

FIGHT OR FLIGHT

Most often, stepping on someone else is reflex; little if any thought is involved. It all goes back to what's called the fight-or-flight response: a set of physical processes that occur in your body whenever you find yourself in a stressful situation.

Millions of years ago your ancestors were wandering the savanna in Africa, the forests of Europe, or the jungles of Asia. Your relative was out there in the wild, looking for nuts and berries, when he came face-to-face with a lion or tiger or Neanderthal. The moment your relative's eyes locked on the hungry predator or competitor, the central and most primitive portion of his brain, called the hypothalamus, sent an emergency message to your adrenal glands.

Within seconds your relative's system is flooded with adrenaline. Suddenly his heart rate doubles or triples. Blood is pumping nutrients into the muscles in his arms and legs. At the same time the capillaries under his skin close up so surface wounds won't result in as much bleeding. His pupils dilate. Your relative's immune and digestive systems shut off. Any waste products are eliminated to get rid of weight that could slow him down. In a flash your frightened primitive ancestor can run faster, jump higher, hit harder, see farther, hear more acutely, and make decisions quicker. He either lunges at the Neanderthal with his sharpened stick—that's the fight response—or he bolts for the nearest cave or tall tree—the flight response.

Revenge is a kind of wild justice, which the more a man's nature runs to, the more ought law to weed it out.

—Francis Bacon

Jump forward a few hundred millennia and you're sitting in a business meeting. The vice president of human resources, with whom you've had more than your share of disagreements, not so subtly implies you're to blame for the delay with the Acme project.

Your body goes through the same process as your primitive ancestor's body. The advanced part of your twenty-first-century brain perceives a potential threat to your job status. But your primitive hypothalamus sends out the old reliable saber-toothed-tiger alarm to your adrenal glands. You feel your heart pumping. You have the urge to go to the bathroom. You break into a sweat. Your senses seem sharper and your actions quicker.

Rather than grabbing a sharp pencil with which to impale your rival, or bolting for the elevator, you either hit back with your own attack on your peer's competence, or you lean back in your seat and curl up into an approximation of the fetal position to protect yourself from the onslaught.

———

You have heard that it was said, An eye for an eye and a tooth for a tooth. But I say to you, Do not resist an evildoer. But if anyone strikes you on the right cheek, turn the other also; and if anyone wants to sue you and take your coat, give your cloak as well.

—Matthew 5:38–40

———

Even though it's not truly a life-threatening situation, your body reacts as if it were. If you experience enough of these "false alarms," you'll end up with one or more stress-related disorders, such as substance addiction, migraine headaches, insomnia, heart disease, high blood pressure, or sexual dysfunction. Your primitive ancestor didn't have that worry. He was either killed or he killed. And even if he ran away, he probably stopped foraging in that area.

In situations where you're unable to respond right away, you may repress the response. If that happens your response just sits there waiting to surface, not just if the exact same situation arises again, but whenever some situation somehow triggers the memory. Your ancestor got it out of his system. But you come home and kick the dog or get back to your office and step on your assistant. Or, perhaps years later, you step on your partner because he says or does something that triggers a memory of something hurtful your father said or did decades before.

By reflexively responding to what you perceive to be an attack with an attack of your own, you step on someone else, whether it's the person you view as a threat or some innocent bystander, and whether the retribution comes immediately or even years later.

STEPPING UP BY GIVING SOMETHING AWAY

My youngest son, Matt, was an all-star hockey player in high school. I used to watch his games with mixed emotions. Mostly, I wanted him to be safe. But I'll admit there were times I wanted him to respond to dirty hits. And at times he'd drop his gloves and end up in the penalty box.

One night during his senior year he and I took in a Philadelphia Flyers game against the Boston Bruins. A shot was deflected and the puck flew into the crowd. Matt stretched and caught it. Now, Matt had always wanted to catch a puck at a game. But when it finally happened, he decided to step up by giving it away.

Sitting behind us were a father and his five-year-old son. It was the first time the little guy had ever been to a hockey game. Matt glanced at the puck and then turned and handed it to the youngster. Everyone sitting in our section started clapping, and people nearby slapped him on the back. I was just a little bit proud of him. Ironically, a friend, Marge Bishop from Massachusetts, telephoned us the next day to tell us they were watching the Bruins game on TV and saw Matt step up by giving the puck to the little kid.

This isn't just an American "cowboy" phenomenon. The culture of premeditated payback is a huge part of ice hockey, the national sport of that most easygoing of nations, Canada. Hit a goaltender, even legally, and you can expect to be attacked in retaliation. Take a cheap shot at a player and either he or one of his teammates will come after you. Often this payback comes in the most overt manner possible: dropping your gloves and openly challenging the offender to a fistfight.

Cultures that encourage stepping on others aren't just centered on pursuits with physical activity. Law schools, which you'd think would look to foster an intellectual, inquiring environment, actually create an aggressive setting.

The book *The Paper Chase* by John Jay Osborn traces the first year in a prestigious law school of a young man named James T. Hart. Based on Osborn's own experiences at Harvard

University Law School, the story centers on the brilliant but brutal professor Charles W. Kingsfield Jr. Infamous for his intellectual and emotional abuse of students, Kingsfield starts the first class of each semester by intentionally humiliating one student in front of his or her peers, ending his assault by handing the victim a coin and saying, "Here is a dime. Go telephone your parents and tell them you will *never* be a lawyer."

Such fictional abuse in an academic environment pales when compared to the kind of real-world abuse that takes place in businesses.

Movie producer Scott Rudin is infamous as the most feared boss in Hollywood and has been referred to as Boss-Zilla. Rudin routinely screams and yells abuse at his assistants. In a recent five-year period he is reported to have gone through more than 250 assistants. He has fired assistants while in a car with them, telling them to take a taxi home. Rudin commonly throws telephones at his staff, prompting assistants to measure the length of phone cords so they can stay out of range. Despite his behavior, positions on his staff are sought-after jobs. Besides the ample networking opportunities, having been one of Rudin's assistants is considered a mark of having what it takes to survive in the brutal world of Hollywood business. If that's not a sign of an industry with an abusive culture, I don't know what is.

THE DOWNFALL OF "CHAINSAW" AL

When Sunbeam Inc. hired Al Dunlap as its CEO in 1996, shares in the company rose 60 percent in one day. That's because

Dunlap was known as a turnaround genius who'd boosted the value of his previous company, Scott Paper, by $6.3 billion in eighteen months. He was the embodiment of aggressive cost-cutting management. When asked about his seeming heartlessness, Dunlap was famously quoted as saying, "If you want a friend, buy a dog."

Upon his arrival at Sunbeam, Dunlap lived up to the reputation that had earned him the nickname Chainsaw Al. By all reports he screamed, harangued, and intimidated. The human resources chief reported he knew things had changed when Dunlap's first expense report included purchases of a bulletproof vest and a handgun. It's easy to see why he thought he'd need those items. His restructuring plan called for the elimination of half of the company's six thousand employees and 87 percent of its products. The result was chaos.

If managers couldn't meet Dunlap's increasingly unrealistic demands, they were terminated. According to company managers, Dunlap threw tantrums, was profane, at times even violent. Under pressure, corners were cut and accounting rules were ignored. Eventually stock analysts began to pick up on what was actually going on. The stock collapsed. Under Dunlap's chain-saw style of leadership the stock went from $53 a share to $6. He was ousted by the board.

Premeditated damage

Premeditatively stepping on someone else is more damaging than a reflexive response—think of how differently the law treats first-degree murder and involuntary homicide. That's not because the victim feels any more pain. It's because someone capable of planning and then carrying out an attack is far more likely to do so again than someone reacting out of reflex. As a result, he is more dangerous to society. Not incidentally, he is also more dangerous to himself since the damage to the soul of such behavior can be incalculable.

Man's capacity for justice makes democracy possible, but man's inclination to injustice makes democracy necessary.

—Reinhold Niebuhr

One reason is, it stifles innovation and clear thinking. People are most often stepped on when there's a disagreement. It's hard to listen to contrarian voices or to dissent unless you've a strong ego. When people realize that if they voice concerns or critiques they'll be stepped on, they stop raising issues. Suddenly a group of otherwise intelligent individuals becomes a pack of yes-men and yes-women. Even as demanding and forceful a leader as General George S. Patton realized dissent needed to be encouraged, not stepped on. He famously once said, "If everyone is thinking alike, someone isn't thinking." When people in a system or organization are afraid of being

stepped on, creativity dies. When they feel free to offer different ideas, innovation blooms.

Another reason premeditatively stepping on someone else
destroys a system is that it can spread like cancer.

The test of a first-rate intelligence is the ability to hold two opposed ideas in the mind at
the same time, and still retain the ability to
function. One should, for example, be able
to see that things are hopeless and yet be
determined to make them otherwise.

—F. Scott Fitzgerald

The vicious cycle

Revenge tends to metastasize inside a company, organization,
or family. Stepping on someone else rarely if ever occurs in a
vacuum: it's just one part of a potentially endless cycle. The
guy who steps up to the plate after a home run gets hit with a
pitch. The next inning his teammate on the mound retaliates.

That hit batsman, a second baseman, charges the mound and connects with a roundhouse right. The benches empty. Players are ejected, fined, and suspended. But later that season the second baseman who charged the mound gets taken out trying to make the pivot on a double-play ball. The next inning the base runner who took out the second baseman gets hit by the pitcher . . . and on and on it goes.

Even indirect retaliation leads to a vicious spiral. Let's go back to that business meeting with your rival, the vice president of human resources. She steps on you. Overflowing with adrenaline, you come back to your office and, in turn, step on your assistant for not having your call list prioritized. Later that afternoon your assistant steps on the woman working at the front desk for not getting a receipt for a package that was picked up. That evening she snaps at her husband for being late for dinner. Nursing his beer and his anger, he yells at their teenage daughter for spending so much time on the telephone. And the next morning at school she talks back to her biology teacher.

Repressed revenge can spread just as far and have even longer-lasting impact. A young woman from a disadvantaged family marries early and starts her family. Her husband abandons her and her children. Angry at her absent husband, frustrated at her inability to care for her family as well as she'd wish, and overwhelmed by the burden of four children at home, she smacks her children whenever they misbehave or talk back or even just react slower than she'd like. Over the years her children grow up and marry in turn. The oldest daughter also marries young and, modeling her mother's behavior, hits her children. The middle two children, a son and a daughter, successfully avoid the family's darker legacies. But the youngest, a son, deals with his frustrations by also smacking his children. Unfortunately, the pattern is apt to keep repeating itself generation after generation. It's the embodiment of the lines from Exodus about "visiting the inequity of the fathers upon the children unto the third and fourth generation."

I suppose you could call Darius McGlockton the father of his company. Darius, forty-eight, graduated near the top of his class in business school and was recruited to join a software firm based in the Southwest. A hard-driving marketing specialist, Darius climbed to the top of that company's sales force within three years. But in another two he was gone, leaving to start a company of his own, largely by poaching talent and customers from his previous employer.

Darius, a former all-American Division II football player, loves competition. He created a sales and marketing company in which each region was a completely autonomous team. Instead of having a research and development division, Darius had a small group he called his talent scouts, who looked for independently owned small software companies whose products fit niche markets. Darius would buy up the small firm, then get his group of sales regions to compete over generating the maximum sales in the shortest period. Rather than looking to extend product life, Darius's plan was to continue to buy up new products and progressively keep squeezing each dry. His sales meetings were free-for-alls, with each regional sales manager encouraged to outdo his peers. Darius promised the highest achiever would get sizable bonuses, while the lowest performer would get terminated.

The ultimate weakness of violence is that it is a descending spiral, begetting the very thing it seeks to destroy. Instead of diminishing evil, it multiplies it. Through violence you may murder the liar, but you cannot murder the lie, nor establish the truth. Through violence you may murder the hater, but do not murder the hate. So it goes. Returning violence for violence multiplies violence, adding deeper darkness to a night already devoid of stars. Darkness cannot drive out darkness; only light can do that. Hate cannot drive out hate: only love can do that.

—Martin Luther King Jr.

In contrast to revenge, which is the natural, automatic reaction to transgression and which, because of the irreversibility of the action process, can be expected and even calculated, the act of forgiving can never be predicted; it is the only reaction that acts in an unexpected way and thus retains, though being a reaction, something of the original character of action.

—Hannah Arendt

Early in his sales meeting for the third quarter, Darius started to give his Northeast and Mid-Atlantic sales managers a hard time. He was startled when, in the midst of a tirade, the usually meek Mid-Atlantic manager interrupted him. Smiling, the manager stood up, closed her binder, and said, "I quit." Before Darius could say anything, the Northeast manager stood up, closed his binder, and said, "So do I. And by the way, we're starting our own company and have signed up those two new software companies you've been pursuing."

"Daddy, Daddy, Daddy"

The building supply company for which Frank Gonzalez, forty-five, works has a far healthier culture than Darius Mc-Glockton's software firm. But that doesn't mean people don't get stepped on. Frank, an outgoing, funny man, jokes about how much he looks like Desi Arnaz. Though he never went to college and actually barely graduated high school, Frank worked his way up from carpenter's assistant to national sales manager for a multimillion-dollar company that manufactures and sells radiant-floor-heating supplies.

Able to deal equally well with contractors, homeowners, and other salespeople, Frank is almost universally loved inside the company. Still, his lack of skill at administrative tasks and with information technology has led to some problems. The comptroller, Beth Jefferson, twenty-eight, a tall, thin, stylish woman, who's normally easy to work with, is a stickler for proper procedures. At nearly every meeting of the leadership group she voices her problems with Frank's inability to keep up with his paperwork and communication. Frank, uncomfortable with computers, verbalizing in a corporate setting, and dealing with a much younger woman who's a peer, never responds in kind to what he perceives as his being stepped on by Beth. He grins and promises to do better. But it doesn't stop there.

Frank and his wife, Marie, are parents to three lovely little girls: Carla, ten, Rose, eight, and Frida, six. They worship their father and, like most young children, can't wait for him to come home from work so they can tell him about their day, ask him to referee disputes, or get his approval for one thing or another. Every day Frank comes home from work he's met with yells of "Daddy, Daddy, Daddy," and three high-pitched, insistent voices vying for his attention. And usually it's music to his ears, grounding him and reminding him of what's important. But on days when there's been a meeting of the leadership team and he's been stepped on by Beth, his reaction is different. He silences the girls with a glare and a loud, angry command to go to their rooms, followed shortly by a hollered attack on Marie.

IT'S IN US ALL

All of us are capable of stepping on others. As human beings, we are imperfect. To transcend our "shadow" sides and begin to step up in life and in work, we first need to acknowledge we're capable of hurting, as well as helping, others. Contemplating this darker part of myself always leads me back to some lines from a wonderful poem called "The Answer," written by Welsh poet R. S. Thomas.

> There have been times
> when, after long on my knees
> in a cold chancel, a stone has rolled
> from my mind, and I have looked
> in and seen the old questions lie
> folded and in place
> by themselves, like the piled
> graveclothes of love's risen body.

"I just can't take it anymore"

Instead of stepping on her children, like Frank Gonzalez, Claudia Jones, thirty-nine, stepped on her boss. A hardworking, skilled project manager, Claudia, a demure brunette, is far more detail-oriented than her immediate supervisor, Victor Francis, forty-nine. Victor, a bit of a dandy, is far better at relating to others, both inside and outside the company. For more than three years Claudia has been frustrated by Victor's lack of appreciation for her skills.

Claudia has been successful in launching and managing the sales of three of the company's most important new products. Yet she feels she hasn't sufficiently been rewarded or appreciated. When she learned of an opening in another division, Claudia decided to go for it. But rather than discussing her intentions with Victor, she waited for him to go on vacation before making her approach, stepping on him, albeit subtly.

Then, when she went in to make her case to Simone Clark, vice president of the division, she stepped on Victor more overtly. When Simone asked why Claudia wanted the job, which was actually a horizontal move rather than a step up, Claudia said she was burned out. Instead of describing how her skills and abilities were a perfect fit for the open position, she said was miserable working for Victor and that if she didn't get a new position, she'd probably leave the company. Simone asked Claudia if she'd talked to Victor about the situation. Claudia admitted she hadn't, saying she thought it wouldn't make a difference.

Simone, taken aback by Claudia's stepping on Victor, nonetheless thought she was the best candidate for the open position. When Victor returned from vacation, Simone called him into her office to tell him about Claudia's attack on him. Under the circumstances, Victor said he'd be glad to get Claudia out of his department. While she landed the new position, Claudia has also landed on Victor's hit list. Simone, though not as vehement, is now also wary of Claudia.

Those who cannot remember the past are condemned to repeat it.

—George Santayana

"We're committed to customer service"

My guess is that my insurance company is now also somewhat wary of me. With one of my sons coming home from military service in Iraq and the other going off to college, I needed to make adjustments to my auto insurance coverage. Because I was in the midst of a busy week and thought the process would be straightforward, I decided to make the call on my cell phone while I was in a taxicab on the way to an appointment. Big mistake.

First, I had to enter everything from my policy number to my mother's maiden name using the keypad on my phone. Then I had to wade through an endless choice of options, none of which applied, before I was told I could press 9 to speak to a customer service representative. After pressing 9, I was put on hold. Every twenty seconds the techno version of a Bach concerto was interrupted by a voice telling me, "We're committed to customer service." The longer I held and the more I heard that obviously false claim, the angrier I got.

When a human voice finally came on the line, I was asked to provide the exact same information I'd entered with the keypad five minutes earlier. After doing that again, I was fuming. When the disinterested voice on the other end asked what she could do for me, I snapped, "For a starter you can stop telling me how much you care about customer service while you're wasting my time on hold." Instead of its eliciting the kind of apology I wanted, she became even more disinterested. "Sorry, sir, what else can I do for you today?" She felt comfortable stepping on me because I was just a disembodied voice, and I felt equally comfortable hitting back. "I want to speak with your supervisor," I barked. After venting to the supervisor, who offered the kind of supplication I craved, and having all my needs efficiently met, I hung up.

How could we all have stepped up?

There's almost never a need to step on someone else. All of us have a choice. We can break the cycle of anger and revenge and striking out and look for other responses. We can instead choose to step up, experience meaning in our life or work, and perhaps also help our company and other people.

Darius McGlockton sowed what he had reaped. By creating a business culture of every man or woman for him- or herself, and encouraging competition rather than cooperation, it was only a matter of time before people turned on him. Darius could have stepped up by working to create a culture of cooperation instead. That needn't mean eliminating competition or giving up on the kind of energy that comes from a sportsmanlike structure. Instead of following the maxim "Winning is everything," he could have followed another adage: "There's no *I* in *team.*"

Rather than taking his workplace frustrations out on his kids when he came home, Frank Gonzalez could have broken the cycle of stepping on others. He might have taken a deep breath and told his daughters, "Daddy needs a time-out." Using language and concepts they understand and giving himself a chance to decompress, Frank could have stepped up and insured that the cycle stopped before it included his children.

PAY IT FORWARD

What would happen if we broke the cycle of stepping on others: if instead of paying back people who do things to us, we paid things forward? That's the question that lies at the heart of the book *Pay It Forward,* written by Catherine Ryan Hyde. In the book, teacher Rueben St. Clair challenges his middle-school students with an extracredit project: think of an idea for world change, and put it into action. Trevor, one of his students, comes up with an exceptional idea:

"If someone did you a favor, something big, something that you could not do on your own, and instead of paying it back, you paid it forward to three people. And the next day, they each paid it forward to three more people. And the day after that those twenty-seven people each paid it forward to three more people. And each day everyone in turn paid it forward to three more people; in two weeks that comes to 4,782,969 people."

Claudia Jones could have stepped up in a couple of ways. She could have spoken to her immediate supervisor about her frustrations and tried to work things out "within the family" before bringing the issue upstairs. Sure, it may have been momentarily satisfying to stick it to her boss. But in the long term it will probably come back to haunt her. Even if she couldn't manage to have that kind of discussion, she could have used the meeting with the department head to promote her qualifications for the new position, and to present a positive picture of what she could bring to the company, rather than a negative picture of her current position.

It wouldn't really have taken much for me to step up in my phone conversation with the insurance company. Sure, the company is in some ways stepping on me and all its other customers by treating us poorly. But repaying mistreatment from them with mistreatment of my own did nothing to improve the situation. I could easily have made my points without being nasty or antagonistic. My attack didn't help me in the least and probably reinforced the customer service representative's negative attitude, making things worse for the next caller. It was easier for me to step on someone whom I didn't have to look in the eye than to take a moment to think about things and instead step up. It would have taken no more effort or time for me to be civil. And perhaps that would have been like a pebble in the water, sending out small but potentially powerful ripples of human kindness.

Stepping on someone comes all too easily to most of us. Whether that's because we give in to our primitive reflexes or to a culture that encourages payback doesn't really matter. What counts is that we're hurting ourselves, our company, and others. It's time to start thinking about what we do before we do it; to realize we have options, and the choices we make have consequences. It's time to step up.

STEPPING UP BY SURRENDERING

On May 10, 1748, John Newton was desperately trying to steer his ship through a violent storm. Born the son of a London merchant in 1725, he first went to sea at the age of eleven and served in the Royal Navy before becoming captain of his own vessel plying the slave trade along the coast of Africa. One day with the storm raging around him and the ship about to sink, Newton exclaimed, "Lord, have mercy upon us." The storm subsided.

Later in his cabin Newton began to believe God had both brought the storm and delivered him from it. By 1755 he'd left the sea and at the age of thirty began to educate himself. Eventually, he was ordained a priest by the Anglican bishop of Lincoln and went on to preach around the British Isles, condemning slavery and all its evils, and composing many hymns of his own. Newton always cited the day of the storm as the date of his submission to a higher power.

While Newton's personal story is intriguing, it's one of his hymns, reportedly representing his thoughts right after that memorable storm, that has ensured his place in history:

Amazing grace! (how sweet the sound)
That sav'd a wretch like me!
I once was lost, but now am found,
Was blind, but now I see.

'Twas grace that taught my heart to fear
And grace my fears reliev'd,
How precious did that grace appear
The hour I first believ'd!

Thro' many dangers, toils and snares,
I have already come.
'Tis grace has brought me safe thus far,
And grace will lead me home.

The Lord has promis'd good to me,
His word my hope secures.
He will my shield and portion be,
As long as life endures.

Yes, when this flesh and heart shall fail,
And mortal life shall cease,
I shall possess, within the veil,
A life of joy and peace.

The earth shall soon dissolve like snow,
The sun forbear to shine,
But God, who call'd me here below,
Will be forever mine.

6

Stepping Up

The purpose of life is not to be happy. It is to be useful, to be honorable, to be compassionate, to have it make some difference that you have lived and lived well.

—Ralph Waldo Emerson

Wake up. Stop sleepwalking through your life and your work. Don't just do what you've always done, what your reflexes tell you to do, what others have done in the past, or what you've been told or taught to do by parents, teachers, or mentors. Rely instead on your mind and soul and heart. Take a deep breath and think about your situation. Be aware of the consequences of your actions, for good or ill, for yourself, for others, and for your company or organization. And take responsibility. Step up.

Stepping up means doing the right thing; making the loving choice, the one that does the most good. It means accepting that you have a responsibility to your family and friends and neighbors; to your coworkers, employees, and customers; and to your company, community, and country.

Throughout my life as a priest I've ministered to hundreds of people who were facing death. Every single one of them, whether the eighty-six-year-old fisherman in Gloucester, Massachusetts, who'd lived a full and active life and was now dying of pneumonia, or the eleven-year-old girl from suburban Philadelphia dying of childhood leukemia who never had a chance to fulfill her potential, asked me one question. Each phrased it differently. But in the final analysis they all asked me the same thing: Did I matter? Did I make a difference? Did I count? In the darkness, when there's nothing but us, our thoughts, and our higher power, that's what we want to know: whether our existence had meaning.

If you step up, if you think about your actions and do your best to make the loving choice, you'll experience meaning in your life and your work. Step up in ways large and small, at work and at home, and when you're facing your mortality, you'll know the answer to the eternal question. Step up and you'll know you made a difference.

Remember that each day, in going through our personal and professional lives, we confront dozens, perhaps hundreds, of situations in which we face choices. In response to each of those situations we make decisions. And every one of those decisions, whatever its apparent import, has consequences.

Throughout this book we've explored many of the choices people make at work and at home, and many of the decisions I've made in my own life. I hope these discussions have led you to think of some of the choices you yourself have made, not just years in the past, but in the hours or days since you started this book.

I try to do the right thing at the right time. They may just be little things, but usually they make the difference between winning and losing.

—Kareem Abdul-Jabbar

BECOME AWARE, DON'T ASSIGN BLAME OR ASSUME SHAME

There are times when all of us stand still, step aside, step back, or even step on someone else. Together we've looked behind those choices to uncover the motivations why we may have made them. Perhaps we stood still in dealing with a spouse because that's what our parents did in similar situations. Maybe we stepped back to block a peer because that's what is encouraged in our organization's culture. Or it could be we gave in to our fight-or-flight instinct and stepped on someone else.

My intention in discussing the potential reasons for our actions wasn't to assign blame to anyone or anything (myself included), nor to shame you for anything you've done. I want us all to get beyond the blame and shame game. Just because your father ignored your mother when she expressed her feelings doesn't make him responsible for your ignoring your own spouse. Just because your company has a cutthroat culture that encourages extreme competition rather than teamwork is no excuse for your sabotaging someone else's project. And just because when you had run-ins with your coach when you were young is no reason for you to scream at your daughter's soccer coach.

You are a mature, thinking adult. Unlike a child, you have the capacity and wisdom to realize you're responsible for your actions and their consequences. Children can't understand that. And neither, apparently, can Larry David. Of course, I'm not referring to Larry David in real life; I mean the character he plays on his television comedy *Curb Your Enthusiasm*. Larry never thinks about what he does. He just does what he feels like doing and says what he feels like saying. He's like a child, or perhaps more appropriately, a human id. In one episode Larry learns that a friend's elderly father was a kamikaze pilot in World War Two. Larry immediately starts asking inappropriate questions: How could he be a kamikaze pilot and still be alive? Did he just miss his target? Or did he get cold feet at the last moment and swerve away? Larry can't see his questions are disturbing his friend, bringing up all sorts of issues for him. Instead he keeps asking questions that he thinks are insightful and funny. Hours later his friend attempts suicide.

Larry doesn't understand that he's responsible for what he says and does. I'm sure you do. In going over the reasons and motivations that may underlie your choices, I've tried to make you more aware of what you might be doing and why. I've tried to become more aware to why I do what I do as well. You see, I think it's that awareness that makes all the difference.

You have many choices. You can choose for-giveness over revenge, joy over despair. You can choose action over apathy. You hold the key to how well you make the emotional ad-justment to your divorce and consequently how well your children will adapt.

—Stephanie Marston

A way of being in the world

Stepping up isn't just a particular type of action. Instead, it's a way of being in the world; one that applies to every aspect of our lives from personal matters to business issues to even our relationship with our higher power.

I can't tell you what you need to do in every situation; no one can. Only you are in position to know all the issues, all the complications, all the factors surrounding the decision you may be facing. That's why only you know what is the right thing to do in your situation. What matters is that you take the time to think, meditate, or pray about what to do. It's that pause for contemplation that makes all the difference and that lets you make a difference in your life. Sometimes it may last just a few seconds. Other times it may require a retreat of a few days' duration. However long that pause lasts, it says you are making an aware choice. It says you've woken up. It says you're stepping up.

———————

The pause that refreshes.

—Coca-Cola advertising slogan

———————

It's the motivation, not the action itself

Though stepping up might mean taking a bold, positive step, such as Teddy Roosevelt leading the charge up San Juan Hill, making a difference doesn't always need to be so overt, active, and physical. Many times, stepping up may actually require you to stand still, step aside, step back, or maybe even step on someone.

If your organization is tearing itself apart in a debate between two courses, both of which you feel are wrong, you could step up by standing still and trying to keep the discussion alive long enough for better alternatives to emerge.

If that fails to happen and the company is on a self-destructive course, you could step up by stepping back and doing what you can to block the path.

Maybe you realize the best thing for the company would be

to retain the services of a young executive whose path to promotion has been blocked. By stepping aside and letting her take the lead, you'd be stepping up as well.

Finally, there may be a time when you need to step on someone to help him in the long term. The subordinate who has repeatedly broken the rules might learn only through punishment of some kind. While you may be stepping on him today, you'd be stepping up for his long-term future. Whatever the tactics you adopt in a given situation, there's always a chance for you to step up and make a difference.

STEPPING UP BY FORGIVING

When I was young, my family lived in Ecuador. It was a fascinating experience. Some of my schoolmates were the children of missionaries. The stories of what had happened to their fathers, and how their families had responded, had a profound impact on my life. In 1955 four missionaries, Nate Saint, Ed McCully, Jim Elliot, and Peter Fleming, launched an effort to help a primitive, isolated tribe in the Ecuadorian rain forest. The tribe called themselves the Huaorani, but were referred to by their neighbors as the Aucas, or savages. They were so violent they were even feared by the famous head-hunting Jivaro tribe, who lived nearby.

After three months of efforts, the four missionaries eventually made tentative contact with the Huaorani. After enlisting the aid of a fifth man, a former paratrooper named Roger Youderian, who had been working with the Jivaros, they decided to make direct contact. Things started well, but at some point there was a misunderstanding and the former para-trooper and four missionaries were all killed by the Huaorani.

But rather than the effort being abandoned, additional missionaries stepped up to take the place of the five who had died. In less than three years, Rachel Saint, sister of Nate Saint, and Elisabeth Elliot, widow of Jim Elliot, stepped up and moved into a Huaorani settlement to practice basic medicine. Six years after that, two of those responsible for the murders actually baptized two of Nate Saint's children, Kathy and Stephen. By 1995, the Huaorani asked Stephen Saint to step up and move to their settlement with his wife and four children to help them develop internal leadership.

The Saint and Elliot families were inspirations to me from an early age, showing me how it was possible to break a cycle of violence by stepping up and doing the loving thing. And to bring my own part of the story full circle, thirty years later while rector in Gloucester, Massachusetts, I was surprised to find Elisabeth Elliot, back in the United States, visiting my congregation.

"What's left to do?"

Michael Macintosh, forty-seven, doesn't know what to do. A barrel-chested widower with thinning black hair and a bushy mustache, Michael has worked hard at raising his son, Stephen. The two have always been close and have been successful at working through all the problems and pitfalls they faced together after the premature death of Naomi, Michael's wife and Stephen's mother. But in the past two years there have been problems.

Stephen, now seventeen, has become increasingly irresponsible. He's gotten into fights, cut classes, been suspended from the football team—and those are just the things Michael knows about. Michael first tried having a heart-to-heart talk with Stephen and offering him positive reinforcement.

Michael told Stephen he'd help him buy a car if he maintained a B average in his junior year in high school and would buy him a new cell phone if he made sure to call and let Michael know where he was at 10 p.m. every night. Stephen ended up with a C, and the few times he did call to let Michael know his whereabouts, it was after 2 a.m. and it was a request for a ride home because he and his friends were all drunk.

When positive reinforcement failed, Michael went negative. He refused to let Stephen use a car. He told him he couldn't go to Florida with his friends for spring break. And he refused to let him work at the after-school job he loved unless his grades got better. None of those efforts worked either.

Angry at Stephen and himself, Michael was distraught. Then, to top matters off, he got a call at 3 a.m. on a Friday night from an old high school friend who is a lieutenant on the local police force. His old friend told him Stephen had been brought in after a drunken brawl among two groups of rival high schoolers. As a favor to Michael, the lieutenant was seeing to it that charges against Stephen were dropped. But he warned Michael this was Stephen's last chance.

Michael said nothing to Stephen on the ride home. That night he cried as he lay in bed wondering what he could do, worrying he was losing his son, feeling he had failed Naomi.

He prayed for help. He asked, "What's left to do?" The next morning he woke Stephen up and asked him to come downstairs. Michael had decided to step up by humbling himself. Rather than sitting opposite Stephen, Michael moved a chair next to him and sat at his side. Instead of telling him what to do, Michael humbled himself by asking Stephen for help. He explained how important Stephen was to him, and how he'd tried everything he knew or could think of to help. Now he was asking Stephen to help him. He started crying. So did Stephen.

Stephen will never be nominated for sainthood. But he did straighten up. He's currently taking classes in a community college and working part-time as a fireman.

Let everything you do be done as if it makes a difference.

—William James

To intervene or not to intervene

Paul Freeman, fifty-four, is as smooth and suave as they come. Of medium height with wavy, sandy hair, Paul sports a year-round tan and dresses as if he'd just stepped out of a Ralph Lauren ad. As communications director of an educational consulting and testing company, he reports directly to the vice president of the company, Lilly Vanderbilt. Lilly, in her early sixties, has been in educational testing her whole working life. A short, birdlike woman, whose assertiveness and temper belie her stature, Lilly takes great pains to neither look nor dress her age. For all her expertise and success, Lilly is uncomfortable with being on center stage. Paul, on the other hand, is a born performer, who thrives in a public spotlight. Together, Paul and Lilly have developed a symbiotic work relationship: Paul performs all the public roles Lilly fears. The problem is he isn't doing his own job well. Paul's communications experience is scant at best. Most of his career was actually spent in sales.

STEPPING UP THROUGH MANIPULATION

In the last few months of Lyndon Johnson's presidency he desperately wanted to extend his incredible civil rights record by nominating the first African American to the Supreme Court. He believed Richard Nixon, who was likely to replace him, was unlikely to name an African American. Johnson's problem was there were no openings on the Court. So he decided to create one.

Johnson approached Ramsey Clark and explained he'd like to name him to be attorney general, but he had a problem. Ramsey Clark's father, Tom Clark, was a Supreme Court justice. Johnson told Ramsey he was afraid he wouldn't be able to name him attorney general because it would be construed as a potential conflict of interest. He asked Ramsey Clark if his father might be ready to retire from the bench.

Justice Clark, eager to help his son, soon retired. Ramsey Clark was named attorney general. And Thurgood Marshall was nominated and quickly confirmed as the first African American Supreme Court justice.

I was first brought into the company by a director of one of the company's other divisions, but was then hired by the board to help work on changing the company's somewhat cutthroat culture. One day there was a knock on the door of the office I was using at the site. The managers of three of the company's communications departments had come by to ask my help. Debbie Harbaugh, thirty-eight, grew up on Manhattan's affluent Upper East Side, attended a prestigious all-girls college, and recently landed the job as press relations officer for one of the company's divisions. Allison Stark, thirty-three, is a rising star in the company. A former clothing designer who dresses more like a downtown artist than a corporate official, Allison had first been brought in as a graphics designer, but worked her way up to become manager of another of the company's press offices. Anita Levy, forty-four, is the veteran of the three. A former newspaper journalist, Anita is a married mother of three whose steady hand on the tiller has helped right what was another division's floundering press relations staff.

As the spokesperson for the trio, Anita told me they were all disgusted with Paul Freeman. His lack of knowledge about communications issues had become an embarrassment and was starting to impact not just them individually, but their departments and staffs. Paul was great at wining and dining and at meetings with outsiders, but when it came to internal matters, he was clearly out of his depth. Debbie explained that Anita had been covering for Paul's ineptness for more than a year, but couldn't continue to do both his job and her own. The three young women had come to me because they knew of Paul's close relationship to Lilly and realized they could never approach her and expect an open mind.

I told the three women I'd get back to them later that afternoon. Before I'd even had a chance to digest all I'd been told, the telephone rang. It was the executive who'd first brought me into the company, who supervised Anita's department. He'd obviously known about the meeting with the three women and was calling to push me to intervene on their behalf. He cautioned that, while Anita was probably too valuable to Paul to be fired, the other two might end up being terminated for their rebellion. That call was shortly followed by calls from the executives who oversaw Debbie's and Allison's departments as well, once again suggesting I go speak with Lilly about Paul's shortcomings and the revolt taking place in his staff.

I hung up the telephone after the third call. With my head spinning, I went outside to buy a cup of coffee, get some fresh air, and give myself a chance to think. Should I intervene on behalf of the three women? Was that the just thing to do, not just for them, but for Paul, Lilly, the directors of the divisions, and the rest of the company? After some reflection I came up with a different path. I realized that for me to do the loving thing for all involved, I had to step up by stepping back and blocking the intervention.

RISK

There's a wonderful piece of writing that's often cited about the importance of assuming risk in life. It's usually unaccredited, but I believe it may have been written by a woman named Janet Rand. You probably know it, but I think it's well worth rereading.

To laugh is to risk appearing the fool.

To weep is to risk being called sentimental.

To reach out to another is to risk involvement.

To expose feelings is to risk showing your true self.

To place your ideas and your dreams before the crowd is to risk being called naive.

To love is to risk not being loved in return.

To live is to risk dying.

To hope is to risk despair.

To try is to risk failure.

But risks must be taken, because the greatest risk in life is to risk nothing.

The person who risks nothing, does nothing, has nothing, is nothing, and becomes nothing.

He may avoid suffering and sorrow, but he simply cannot learn, feel, change, grow or love.

Chained by his certitude, he is a slave; he has forfeited his freedom.

Only the person who risks is truly free.

I brought the three women back to my office for another meeting. I asked them what they would want if they were Paul.

After some hesitation, Anita admitted that if she were Paul, she'd want to know how everyone felt and be given a chance to repair the damage. I agreed and asked them to step up by stepping aside. I knew, because I had set it up weeks earlier, that the entire communications staff had a strategic retreat scheduled later that month. I asked Debbie, Allison, and Anita to work with me in structuring the retreat's agenda to give everyone a safe space to vent and also give Paul a chance to turn things around. They agreed.

Next I phoned back all three directors. I told each I wasn't going to intervene on their employees' behalf and explained the course the three women and I had charted out. None of the directors were particularly pleased with my choice. I could tell they had all seen me as a useful tool to eliminate someone who had been a thorn in their sides and might be competition for further advancement. Knowing the speed with which "secrets" spread around the organization, I asked all three directors to step up by standing still and doing nothing until the retreat was over.

The retreat didn't go as well as I'd hoped. Despite the best efforts of the women to be diplomatic, and my own attempts to facilitate a way for Paul to restore and redeem himself, he didn't react well. He began by denying there was a problem, then quickly shifted to an aggressive counterattack on those who dared to confront him. Given a chance to step up, he didn't.

That left me with little choice but to go to Lilly myself. Two days after the retreat I was in her office, explaining that something was going on that she needed to know, and deal with, if she wanted to maintain her credibility. Without using names I told her how Paul's staff had come to me asking for help. I told about how the directors had corroborated the initial complaints, and how the retreat had made it clear Paul had no support in the department, but showed no realization that he needed to step up and do something about it. Lilly went through the same process as Paul at the retreat, moving from denial to anger at the messenger. I weathered Lilly's attack and told her that for the staff, for the company, for Paul, and for herself she needed to step up by stepping on Paul. A month later Paul was "promoted" to assistant vice president, reporting directly to Lilly. Anita was named to take his place as communications director.

It's not what you do once in a while, it's what you do day in and day out that makes the difference.

—Jenny Craig

Could the same thing have happened, but a lot sooner, if I had intervened directly when the three women first approached me? Perhaps the outcome would have been the same, but I don't think it would have had the same effect or impact. Stepping up and experiencing meaning isn't just about end results, it's also about the way we get there. By my stepping back, the women stepping aside, the directors standing still, and Lilly's eventually stepping on Paul, everyone, including Paul, had a chance to take responsibility. Everyone was able to make a difference, to experience meaning, in a way that enhanced life, and that was values-driven, even if it was long and painful. That's how an organization heals itself and becomes a place where people want to work.

Stepping up by stepping down

Sometimes, stepping up might seem like surrendering rather than rising to the occasion. That was certainly true for Herve Fuentes. Herve, a fifty-four-year-old former college professor, had been named deputy mayor of a major city. Since his academic specialty was labor-management relations, Herve had been given responsibility for negotiations between the city and its unionized employees. After a couple of bitter strikes I was called in to provide him with leadership coaching and help him reexamine and, if necessary, reorganize his department.

During our coaching sessions I was struck by how miserable Herve seemed. He had dark circles under his eyes. He looked haggard and often seemed on the verge of tears. One afternoon, during a break, I asked Herve what he liked to do most. He told me he loved going on motorcycle trips with his son. I asked him where he'd gone on his most recent trip. He looked at me sadly and told me he hadn't been on a trip for so long he couldn't even remember.

After a few weeks of discussions it was clear that major work was needed to straighten out the department. When this dawned on Herve, he looked as if he'd been sentenced to life in prison. Over an early dinner one evening I told him I was concerned about him. I explained that he seemed terribly depressed and I was afraid he might be heading toward serious health problems.

Herve admitted that he dreamed of quitting, but didn't want to let everyone down. After a few more conversations it dawned on Herve that he would actually be letting everyone down by staying in the job. He was letting down his coworkers and superiors because he was doing a job for which he no longer felt enthusiasm. He was letting down his family by spending little time with them and not taking care of his own health. Finally, he was letting himself down by not doing all he could to be happy. Within a month Herve stepped up by stepping down and handing in his resignation.

———

In matters of truth and justice, there is no difference between large and small problems, for issues concerning the treatment of people are all the same.

—Albert Einstein

———

Little things can make a big difference

Stepping up doesn't have to be a monumental act. Minor actions can have major consequences; maybe not in the short term, but perhaps in the long term. Marian Wright Edelman, president and founder of the Children's Defense Fund, has said, "We must not, in trying to think about how we can make a big difference, ignore the small daily differences we can make which, over time, add up to big differences that we often cannot foresee."

Surprising your assistant by bringing him a cup of coffee and a doughnut on a rainy Tuesday morning when you know he worked late the day before can result in more than just a smile; it could be just the morale boost that keeps him working his hardest. That's just as much stepping up as it is when you give up your family vacation plan and instead travel to visit an angry client who's about to pull her account and send your company into a cash crisis.

Never underestimate the importance of little things you do. One day a middle-aged man was walking along a beach on a lovely tropical island. A powerful corporate executive, he was vacationing on the island, trying to recuperate and recharge. As he strolled down the shore, he saw up ahead a young teenage native of the island. The young man was picking up starfish that had been beached and tossing them back into the ocean. Coming abreast of the young islander, the executive stopped to chat. "Why are you tossing the starfish back in the ocean?" he asked. "If they're stranded on the beach when the sun comes up, they'll die," the youngster explained. The executive looked back along the shoreline he'd already traveled, then glanced ahead to the miles of beach stretching out ahead. There appeared to be thousands of starfish along the length of the beach. Thinking he'd offer some sagacious advice, the executive pointed out all the starfish to the islander: "There are thousands, maybe tens of thousands, of starfish on the beach. How can what you're doing make any difference?" The young man looked sad for a moment, then glanced down at the starfish he was still holding. Suddenly he smiled and tossed it into the ocean, saying, "Well, it makes a difference to this one."

We the willing, led by the unknowing, are doing the impossible for the ungrateful. We have done so much, with so little, for so long, we are now qualified to do anything with nothing.

—Mother Teresa of Calcutta

The importance of little things is just as true for organizations as it is for individuals or starfish. Giving employees time off to take part in a school bake sale sends as strong a message as the company becoming a sponsor for a public television series. The smile and welcoming manner of a receptionist can reverberate throughout an entire company, working its way to the bottom line. Former New Jersey governor Christie Todd Whitman once joked, "Anyone who thinks that they are too small to make a difference has never tried to fall asleep with a mosquito in the room."

Remember: no blame, no shame

Just as you shouldn't blame others for your own behavior, you also shouldn't blame them for not stepping up themselves. Don't do the right thing, then lord your actions over others. We're all on individual journeys to awareness, and each organization is on its own path as well. There's a wonderful moment in Harper Lee's novel *To Kill a Mockingbird* in which the young girl Scout recounts advice from her father: "Atticus was right. One time he said you never really know a man until you stand in his shoes and walk around in them." You don't know all that's going on in other people's lives, so don't assume to judge them.

And don't judge yourself too harshly either. Believe me, even once you've absorbed the stepping-up message, there will still be times when you don't measure up. None of us is perfect and no company is perfect. At times we all fall short of the ideal. I try my hardest to live out the message I teach to my clients, both in my personal life and my work. But lots of times I fall short.

What do I do when that happens? I try to figure out why. Not so I can assign blame or shame, but so I can learn from the insight and try to do better the next time. I know I'll keep stumbling as long as I live. I also know the best I can do is to keep doing my best. Instead of blaming others for failing to step up, or being ashamed of not stepping up yourself, forgive them and forgive yourself. Then try to help them and yourself do better the next time.

Whenever I think about falling short in trying to step up, I remember a wonderful story. I don't know if it's really true, but it's a great story nevertheless. It's February 25, 1956, and Soviet leader Nikita Khrushchev has just delivered a historic speech in front of the Politburo denouncing Joseph Stalin for being a genocidal despot. In gruesome and excruciating detail he recounts the decades of purges and mass deportations and pogroms. When Khrushchev ends, he's met by stunned silence from the audience of party apparatchiks and bureaucrats. Then the room fills with simultaneous boos and cheers and applause and denunciations. One voice breaks through the cacophony. "Comrade Khrushchev," a man yells from the back of the hall. "Where were you when all this was happening? What were you doing when all this was going on?" The crowd falls instantly silent. Khrushchev, calmly and with no animosity, addresses the darkened room: "I can't see you. Will the comrade who asked those questions please stand up so I can see him?" Tension grips the audience. No one rises. Khrushchev waits for a few moments, then smiles. "Well, comrade, whoever you are, you now have your answer. Back then, I was in the same place you are now."

STEPPING UP BY SACRIFICING MATERIAL SUCCESS

An honors student and undersize linebacker at Arizona State, Pat Tillman was a long-shot 226th pick in the 1998 NFL draft by the Arizona Cardinals. Becoming an outstanding NFL safety, and starring for three seasons, Tillman was then offered a new $3.6 million contract in 2001, but turned it down. He explained that rather than continuing his football career, he was going to enlist in the U.S. Army in response to the September 11 attacks.

Avoiding all contact with the news media, who were clamoring for his story, Tillman and his brother Kevin, a minor league baseball player, completed advanced Ranger training, were assigned to the Seventy-fifth Ranger Regiment, and were deployed as part of Operation Iraqi Freedom in 2002. Tillman was subsequently deployed to Afghanistan, where, on April 22, 2004, he was killed in action.

Tillman's stepping up defied stereotypes. Initially a poster boy of the right and demonized by the left as a "misled idiot," it was soon revealed he disapproved of the war in Iraq while supporting the war in Afghanistan, supported John Kerry in the 2004 presidential election, and was an avid reader of leftist author Noam Chomsky. The cause of Tillman's death—friendly fire—was initially covered up by the military and kept from his family and the public, reportedly for public relations reasons.

RISK AND REWARD

Stepping up always involves risk. Rarely is it the kind of mortal risk Khrushchev would have faced had he confronted Stalin, but it can be a tough, uphill struggle. Tom Brokaw has said, "It's easy to make a buck. It's a lot tougher to make a difference."

I've told you I'm experienced at guiding canoe trips along rivers. I may not know the river that runs near your home or vacation site. That means I can't tell you exactly what you'll face and where. But because I know rivers, I can safely tell you some things. You'll likely face some rapids. There will probably be some rocks and maybe some white water. You're also apt to find yourself in some eddies. And I can almost guarantee you'll face some surprises.

What's true for a river trip is also true for your journey toward stepping up and experiencing meaning. It isn't going to be easy to take the time to make loving choices. People could become angry at you for not doing what they expect, or what you've done in the past. They could lash out because subconsciously they feel embarrassed they haven't stepped up, or because they think you're showing them up. But that doesn't mean you shouldn't keep stepping up. It has been said that there are two types of people who will tell you that you cannot make a difference in this world: those who are afraid to try themselves, and those who are afraid that you will succeed.

Step up at work and you may antagonize some of your coworkers who'd rather still not shake things up. Step up at home and you risk alienating some of your family and friends who are comfortable with the way things are. Stepping up represents real change, for people and for organizations. And change isn't easy. D. H. Lawrence wrote, "The world fears a new experience more than it fears anything. Because a new experience displaces so many old experiences." In fact, many people respond to change the same way they grieve, with reflexive denial and anger, because whatever is being changed is, in effect, dying.

It won't be easy for you to step up. But it will be worth it. The flip side of the risk is the reward. And this truly is a priceless reward. I believe one of the reasons we're put on this earth is to be of service to others.

STEPPING UP BY PERSEVERING

Dr. David Livingstone was perhaps the most celebrated and beloved missionary in history and is one of my personal heroes. Exploring and spreading the Gospel, the Scottish medical missionary traveled more than twenty-nine thousand miles in Africa. After years of selfless stepping up, at 4 a.m. on May 1, 1873, his friends and followers heard an unusual noise coming from his hut in the central-African village of Ulala. They lit a candle and entered to find him dead on his knees. Faced with the death of their hero, they decided to step up.

Led by Chuma and Susi, who had been Livingstone's faithful African companions for more than thirty years, they knew what they had to do. They decided to pay homage to him with one last act of devotion. They embalmed his body by filling it with salt and leaving it to dry in the sun for two weeks. Knowing their love for him was shared by his native country, they resolved to carry him home. They wrapped the corpse in the bark of a Myonga tree, around which they sewed heavy sailcloth. They then tied the body to a long pole so it could be carried by two men. Bringing his papers and possessions as well, Chuma,

Susi, and the others headed for Zanzibar, more than a thousand miles away.

The small caravan crossed hostile terrain, passing through the lands of tribes who were horrified by the dead. They persevered knowing this was the last service they could give to their beloved Livingstone, whom they called "the white man who didn't take slaves." It took more than nine months, but they eventually presented Livingstone's body to the British consul in Zanzibar. The body was ultimately buried in the nave of Westminster Abbey. However, one part of him was left behind. Before they launched on their epic journey, Susi and the others removed Livingstone's heart and, fittingly, buried it under a mpundu tree in Ulala.

We have been given the potential to make a difference; the opportunity to step up. That can be as simple as smiling at a stranger, or as complex as making sure an organization deals with an abusive executive in a manner that helps him, his peers, and the company. I believe that to feel fulfilled as human beings we need to fully live our potential; we need to step up. The Hall of Fame outfielder Roberto Clemente, who died New Year's Eve, 1972, while on a humanitarian mission to earthquake-ravaged Nicaragua, once said, "Any time you have an opportunity to make a difference in this world and you don't, then you are wasting your time on earth."

Time is wasting. Step up!

Acknowledgments

Acknowledgments are a difficult matter for the writer. The reason for this, at least for me, is that one inevitably leaves someone off the list who has made a significant contribution to the book and/or to the author's inspiration to write the book. So, I first want to acknowledge those of you who have helped me create *Stepping Up,* and who belong by name on this page. But for reasons unknown to me, your name may not be found in the acknowledgments to follow. Please know I acknowledge you and ask your forgiveness for the omission.

Those I do remember and want to honor and thank: first my family, sons John and Matt, for giving their father the benefit of the doubt. My brother, Dan, who never fails to step up for those in need, my mother, Christine, because she never gives up, and my father, Peter (RIP), because he did his best no matter what the challenges.

I give thanks to and for the following: Mark Levine, without whom this book could not have been written. Mark never lost sight of the message or the meaning. Barbara Bruns, one of the best friends and colleagues I'll always treasure. She has never stopped believing in me and the purpose of *Stepping Up*.

Friends and encouragers: Gene Stone, David Strawbridge, Lisa Hahn, Ian Jackman, Jim Grohl, Dr. Brian Saltzman, Rick Busch, Dr. Philip Watt and family, Don Weisberg, Gary Green, David Naggar, Andrew Weber, Rossana Rosado, Whitney Cookman, who always tries to make a difference: Ginny Felton, Chip Gibson, Barbara Green Gyde, Madeline McIntosh, Jenny Frost, my friends on 16E: Heejin, Casey, Corey, Heather, Nicole, Adele, Brian, Ian, Rebecca, Helen, and others: Michael Rodriguez, and very importantly, The Gainesville Nerve Center, including Dr. Herb Wagemaker: you all know who you are. If not, I'll track you down and make sure you know. Also, Josh, Annette, Phyllis, Peter, Shaye, Lauren, Steve, Kathy, Sheryl, Dr. and Mrs. Michael Hattwick.

Cathy Price, for more than I can say or write, and to my agent, Richard Pine, who knows it when he sees it. I hope I can live the discipline that will make him proud. One of my best friends and supporters, Jack Lusk. He believed in me when others were too busy finding excuses to let go. Asaf Shakham, Jake Willing, Violet Mendoza, Kathryn Matushak, my mentor and guide, Jungian Analyst Dr. Aldon Josey, plus Chris Hart, John Chidiac, Jim Cappalino, and Peter Davidson, who gave me a place to start, and Jean, Mark, and Tim. Special thanks to Beryl Needham-Palmucci, who "made" me write this book and to Dr. Debra Jaliman.

I give thanks for all my clients, and especially my friends at Random House, Inc., who have allowed me to "practice my craft" for and with them, accompanied by a particularly unique set of tools: cultural architecture, leadership development, executive coaching, postmerger divisional and departmental integration, conflict management, counseling, mediation, friendship, and every other category of life and work we have done together. You are too many to name and so many more of you I would leave out. You know who you are.

And finally to HarperCollins/CollinsBusiness: Leah Spiro, friend and former editor. Steve Hanselman, who saw the possibility; Joe Tessitore, who said *he* would have bought it; Marion Maneker, who is making it happen; Alex Scordelis, the go-between with a great future; Larry Hughes, Angie Lee, Andrea Rosen, Libby Jordon, Felicia Sullivan, and the great CollinsBusiness team. I'll always remain grateful. Pax Domini!